WHOLE LIFE
MAKEOVER WORKBOOK

for Women

AURORA NETWORK

AURORA
PUBLISHING

Published by Aurora Publishing,
a division of Aurora Network

ISBN: 979-8-9941561-0-0

Editing, design, and layout by Aurora Publishing.

Printed in the United States of America.

For information, permissions, or special orders, contact:
Aurora Publishing
www.AuroraNetwork.Life

To our beloved sisters in Christ,

This workbook is lovingly dedicated to you. The women who dare to dream, who seek God's purpose, and who are ready to embrace God's very best for her life. May each page remind you of your worth, your calling, and the incredible journey God has set before you.

We believe in your strength, your resilience, and the unique light you bring to the world. As you walk through these exercises, know you are not alone. We are cheering you on, praying for you, and celebrating every step of your transformation.

With love,
The Aurora Network

About Us

Aurora Network is a faith-driven community dedicated to empowering Christian women to live with purpose, passion, and renewed confidence. We believe every woman is uniquely called and deeply loved by God, right where she is, but that His love is far too great to leave her unchanged.

Through coaching, mentorship, and Christ-centered resources, Aurora Network meets women in every season of life. Our team of certified coaches and mentors walks alongside you, offering encouragement, practical tools, and biblical wisdom to help you break through barriers and step boldly into your God-given calling.

We are passionate about creating spaces, both in person and online, where women can experience restoration, discover their strengths, and grow in faith. Whether you're seeking clarity, healing, or a fresh start, Aurora Network is here to support you on your journey to whole life transformation.

You are seen. You are loved. You are called. And we're honored to walk this path with you.

Learn more or connect with us at www.AuroraNetwork.Life.

Haven't Taken the Free Assessment Yet?

Before you continue, take a moment to complete the Christian Women's Life Assessment.
It only takes a few minutes, and your personalized results will give you clarity on which areas need the most attention right now.

This assessment will serve as a helpful guide alongside this workbook, helping you focus your energy, track your growth, and get the most from your makeover journey.

Access your free assessment here or scan the code below and get your results.
https://auroranetwork.life/seven-days-to-a-new-you

TABLE OF CONTENTS

PART FIVE: THE OVERLOADED OVERCOMER PATH

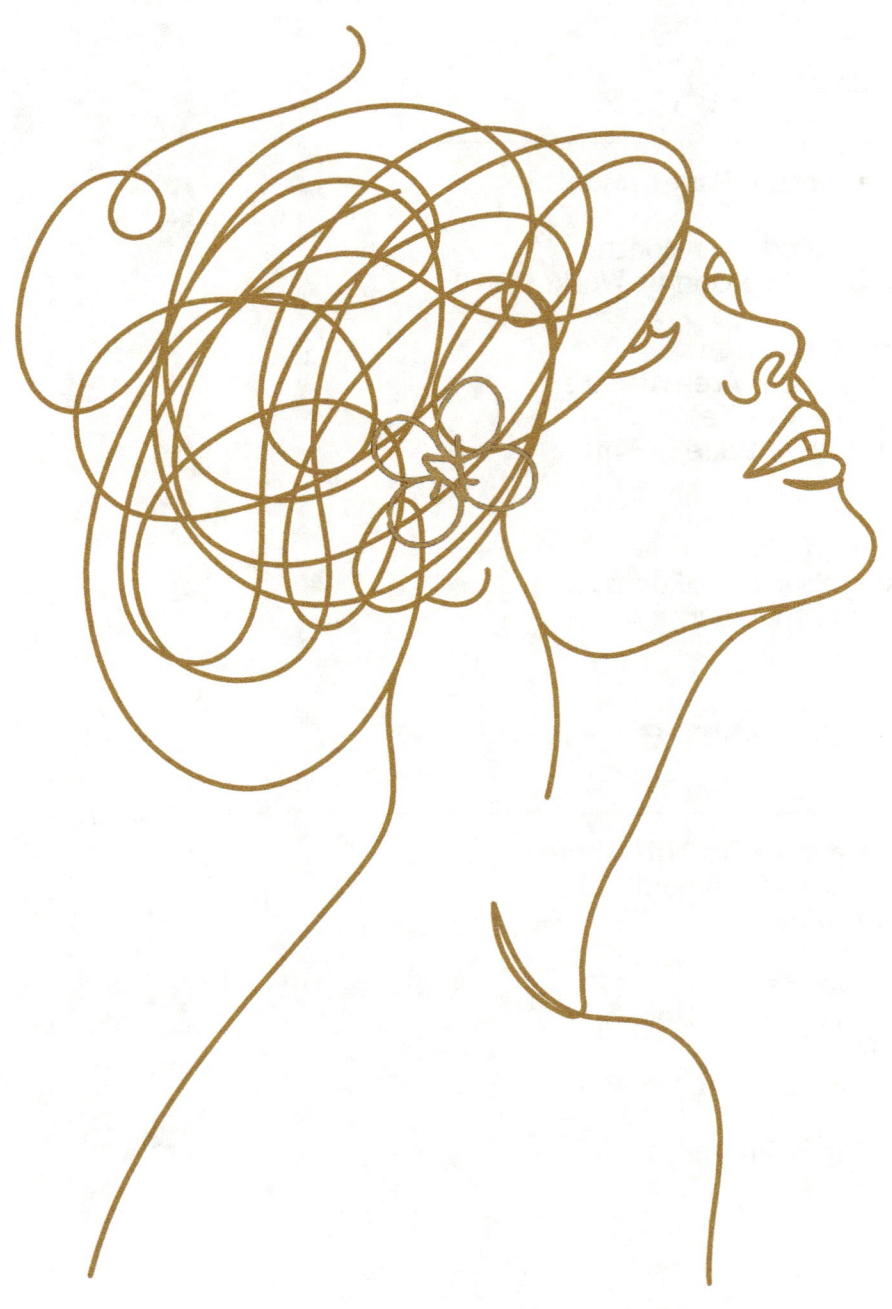

Introduction

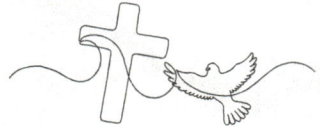

You are here because you know you were created for more than survival mode.

You love God. You care about your people. You carry a lot.
And somewhere in the middle of all of that, you've felt a tug in your spirit that says, "There has to be a better way to live than this."

This workbook is your invitation into that "better way"—not a perfect life, not a Pinterest life, but a whole-life makeover with God at the center.

We're going to look at the big picture of your life:
- Faith – your relationship with God and your identity in Christ
- Health – your body, energy, rest, and emotional well-being
- Finances – your stewardship, generosity, and money mindset
- Relationships – your connections, communication, and boundaries

This is not about perfection. It's about alignment—bringing your everyday life into closer agreement with who God is and who He says you are.

Over the next 7 days, you're going to:
- Get clear on where you're most stuck
- Invite God into that specific area
- Choose one realistic focus
- Set a simple, grace-filled plan in motion

Those first 7 days are your jumpstart—your reset button. But they're not the end of the story. They're the beginning of a longer, gentler, and more sustainable journey.

From here, we'll welcome you into this journey, show you how to use this workbook so it actually serves you, and ground everything in grace, pace, and progress—so you don't burn out trying to "do it right."

Then we'll step into Part One: Foundations for Lasting Change, where we'll start doing the inner work that makes outer change possible.

WELCOME, BUSY BUT CALLED WOMAN

If you're holding this workbook, it's probably because you're tired of feeling like your life is running you instead of you - together with God - intentionally leading your life.

You love Jesus.
You care about your people.
You carry a lot.

You are busy; but you are also called.

You're not just managing tasks; you're carrying assignments from Heaven:
- To love the people God has placed in your life
- To steward the gifts He's put in you
- To reflect Jesus in your corner of the world

The tension you feel, that pull between your responsibilities and your desire to grow, is not a sign that you're failing. It's a sign that you're awake.

GOD SEES
Your Season

God is not asking you to live someone else's life. He sees:
- The kids, the caregiving, the job, the ministry, the business
- The late nights, early mornings, and hidden sacrifices
- The quiet "yes" you give Him in the middle of laundry, emails, and errands

PSALM 139:1–3

*"You have searched me, Lord, and you know me.
You know when I sit and when I rise; you perceive my thoughts from afar.
You discern my going out and my lying down; you are familiar with all my ways."*

This workbook is not here to add guilt or another impossible standard. It's here to help you walk with God inside the busy, messy, beautiful, full life you actually have. And guide you to a deeper sense of fulfillment in all that you're doing.

YOU ARE
Not Behind

You may feel like:
- "I should be further along by now."
- "I've started so many things and not finished."
- "Other women seem to be doing this better."

But in God's Kingdom, you are not behind. You are right on time for what He wants to do in you now.

You are not behind.
You are not too much.
You are not too late.

This is your starting line.

Journaling Prompt

Where have you believed the lie that you're "behind" in your faith, health, finances, or relationships?

_____

_____

_____

_____

_____

_____

_____

_____

What might it sound like if Jesus spoke truth over that area instead?

_____

_____

_____

_____

_____

_____

_____

_____

THIS JOURNEY IS FOR
Real Women

Here, we're not just talking about one piece of your life in isolation. We're looking at the big picture of who you are and what you carry:

- The Weary Warrior – Health & Wellness
- The Hidden Heroine – Personal Development & Purpose
- The Hungry Heart – Faith Life
- The Stretched Steward – Finances
- The Pouring-From-Empty Giver – Relationships

And for some of us, it feels like all of the above (The Overloaded Overcomer).

This workbook is designed for busy Christian women—women with real responsibilities, real schedules, and real limitations. You won't find complicated systems or unrealistic expectations here. Instead, you'll find:

- Gentle, clear guidance
- Small, doable steps
- Space to hear from God
- Practical tools to build habits that actually stick

You don't need to be "ready" in some perfect way. You just need to be willing.

Your willingness + God's faithfulness = a powerful partnership for transformation.

YOUR "WHY" FOR
This Season

Before we go any further, pause and ask:
- Why am I here, in this workbook, in this season?
- What am I longing for that I haven't even said out loud?

Your Personal "Why" Statement

"In this season, I am choosing to show up for my growth because..."

_____

_____

_____

_____

_____

_____

_____

_____

_____

_____

_____

_____

_____

_____

_____

HOW TO USE THIS WORKBOOK

This workbook is meant to be used.

You don't have to fill out every page perfectly. You don't have to do it in order. You don't have to wait for the "right" time. You simply have to start.

This is meant to be a tool you come back to, a place where you and God meet on paper.

WHAT THIS Workbook Includes

You'll find:

- **Teaching sections:** short, Scripture-based narratives to frame each topic
- **Journaling prompts:** questions to help you process with God
- **Exercises and assessments:** practical tools to clarify where you are and where you're going
- **Goal-setting frameworks:** especially in Part One, to help you move from insight to action
- **Weekly and monthly check-in pages:** to help you track progress over time and notice God at work

You do not have to use every single piece perfectly for this to be powerful. Think of it as a buffet: there are key things you'll want to eat regularly, and some you'll use more in certain seasons.

Start with Your Assessment Result (If You Have One)

If you've taken the Aurora assessment, you've already identified your primary pain point in this season. Your result will point you toward one of these:

- **The Weary Warrior** – Health & Wellness
- **The Hidden Heroine** – Personal Development & Purpose
- **The Hungry Heart** – Faith Life
- **The Stretched Steward** – Finances
- **The Pouring-From-Empty Giver** – Relationships
- **The Overloaded Overcomer** – Whole-Life Overload

You'll use that result as your starting focus area.

If you haven't taken the assessment yet, you can either pause and do that first, or simply choose the area that feels most painful or pressing right now.

CHOOSE ONE PRIMARY *Focus Area*

Even though this workbook touches all the key areas of your life, real change happens when you focus.

For the next 7 days, you'll zoom in on one primary area. That doesn't mean the other areas don't matter; it just means you're giving yourself the gift of clarity and simplicity.

You'll be guided to:

- Clarify a God-centered vision for that area
- Set one main focus
- Create tiny, realistic habits that move you toward that vision

After those first 7 days, you'll have a clear starting plan you can continue for the next several weeks so the changes can actually take root.

SUGGESTED *Rhythm*

Option A – Weekly Deep Dive	*Option B – 10–20 Minutes a Day*

• 1 day per week (45-60 minutes):
    ○ Read a section
    ○ Complete the main exercise
    ○ Journal through 2-3 prompts
 	
 • 1 shorter check-in (10-15 minutes):
    ○ Review goals
    ○ Adjust for the week ahead
	• Day 1-2: Read the teaching section
	
	 • Day 3-4: Do the exercise/assessment
	
	 • Day 5-6: Journal through prompts
	
	 • Day 7: Rest, pray, and review

Which rhythm feels most realistic for you in this season?

☐ Weekly deep dive   ☐ Daily small steps   ☐ A combination

"My plan for this season is…"

_____

_____

_____

_____

_____

_____

_____

HOW THE PARTS *Fit Together*

Roadmap for the reader:

- Introduction – Welcome, expectations, and heart posture

- Part One: Foundations for Lasting Change
  - Why change feels hard (and why you're not broken)
  - How God transforms us from the inside out (renewing your mind, identity in Christ)
  - How to set gentle, doable goals and build habits that last

Later sections (if included in your full project) can go deeper into each area:

Faith | Health | Finances | Relationships

We start with foundations because without them, any change you make will feel temporary and fragile. With them, your growth becomes sustainable.

YOUR SPACE *with God*

Treat this workbook as a sacred space:
- Bring your Bible, a pen, and an open heart.
- Expect the Holy Spirit to highlight certain phrases, questions, or verses.
- Write in the margins. Circle, underline, star what stands out.
- Capture prayers, ideas, and even frustrations. God can handle all of it.

Journaling Prompt

Where will you most likely use this workbook? (Kitchen table, favorite chair, car during pickup line, etc.)

_____
_____
_____
_____
_____
_____
_____
_____
_____
_____

What small ritual could you add to make it feel like "meeting with God"? (Candle, worship music, favorite mug, etc.)

_____
_____
_____
_____
_____
_____
_____
_____
_____
_____

WHY 7 DAYS, AND WHY YOU'LL GO BEYOND THEM

You might be wondering, "If this is called '7 Days to a Whole-Life Makeover,' why are there pages for weeks and months?"

Because the first 7 days are about:
- Waking up to where you are and getting radically honest with yourself
- Choosing your focus
- Inviting God into that area
- Designing a simple, realistic plan
- Taking your first few small, courageous steps

Those 7 days are like clearing the clutter off the table so you can actually see what you're working with. They create momentum, hope, and clarity.

But research on habit formation and behavior change, and real life, tell us something important:
- Most people need at least a few weeks of consistent practice for a new habit to feel natural.
- Deeper, more automatic habits often take 60-90 days or more to really stick.

You don't need to remember the numbers; you just need to remember this:

> *Seven days is your jumpstart.*
> *The next several weeks are where your new life takes root.*

So this workbook is designed to:

- Give you a clear, powerful 7-day reset, and
- Equip you with the tools, pages, and prompts you need to keep going long enough for real, lasting change.

You're not failing if you still need this after 7 days. You're being wise.

As you move forward, there are three words I want you to carry with you through this whole process: grace, pace, and progress.

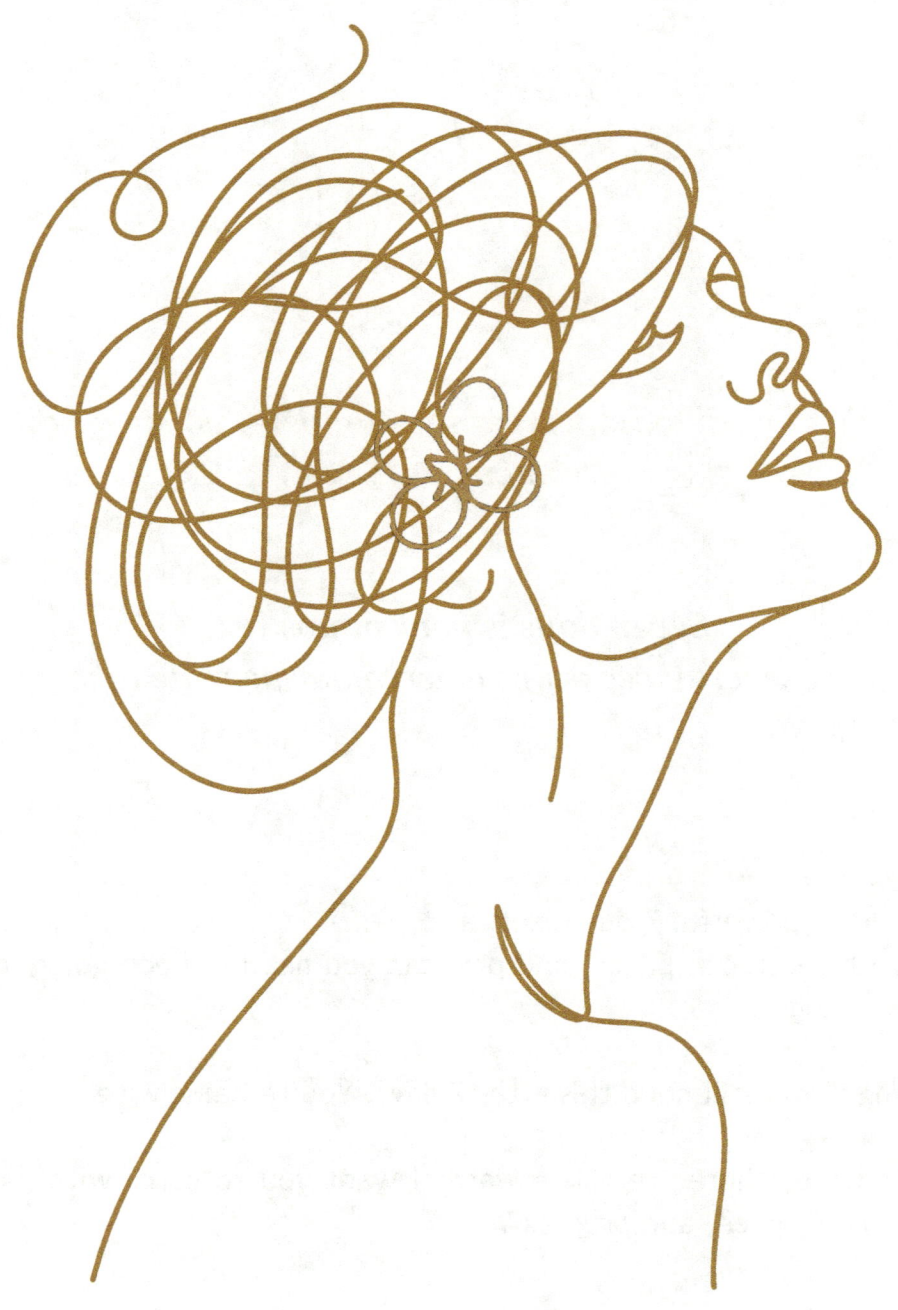

PART ONE:

Foundations for lasting change

Look back with honesty, not shame: when you've tried to change your life before, what patterns, excuses, or fears have pulled you off track or caused you to stop showing up for yourself?

_____

_____

_____

_____

_____

_____

_____

_____

This section is all about what happens inside you as you grow.

Before we talk about specific habits in faith, health, finances, and relationships, we need to understand:
- Why change feels hard (and why you're not broken)
- How God transforms you from the inside out, starting with identity
- How to walk this journey with grace instead of perfectionism

These foundations will make everything you do next more sustainable, gentle, and effective.

As a woman who is serious about growth, what specific commitments will you make—with God's help—to walk this journey differently this time?

_____

_____

_____

_____

_____

_____

_____

_____

_____

WHY CHANGE FEELS HARD
(AND WHY YOU'RE NOT BROKEN)

Change is not hard because you're weak, lazy, or "bad at follow-through."

Change is hard because your brain, your body, and your past experiences are wired to keep you in what feels familiar—even when that familiar place is not healthy or holy.

This chapter will help you understand what's going on under the surface so you can work with how God designed you, not against it, and walk this journey with grace, pace, and progress instead of perfectionism and shame.

YOUR BRAIN *on Change*

God designed your brain to keep you alive and conserve energy. That means your brain loves:

- Predictable routines
- Familiar patterns
- Automatic habits

When you try to change something, start a new habit, break an old pattern, show up differently in some area of your life, your brain often responds with:

- Resistance ("Let's do it later.")
- Doubt ("This won't work.")
- Discomfort ("This feels weird and hard.")

That doesn't mean you're broken. It means your brain is doing what it's always done, trying to keep you safe in what it already knows.

ROMANS 12:2

"Do not conform to the pattern of this world, but be transformed by the renewing of your mind.
Then you will be able to test and approve what God's will is—His good, pleasing and perfect will."

Transformation is not just about willpower. It's about renewing your mind—changing the patterns of thought that drive your choices.

FAMILIAR VS. *Faithful*

Many of the patterns you're living in right now are familiar, but not necessarily faithful.

Familiar might look like:

- Stress eating or skipping meals
- Avoiding your bank account
- Saying "yes" when you want to say "no"
- Numbing out with your phone instead of praying or resting
- Staying in cycles of people-pleasing, overworking, or self-criticism

Faithful looks like:

- Honoring your body as God's temple
- Facing your finances with God instead of hiding from them
- Setting boundaries that protect what God has entrusted to you
- Choosing to sit with God, even for a few minutes, instead of numbing out
- Responding from your identity in Christ instead of old labels and fears

Your brain will often choose familiar over faithful unless you intentionally partner with God to create new patterns.

Journaling Prompt

- *In each area (faith, health, finances, relationships), what is one familiar pattern that is not actually faithful?*

_____

_____

_____

_____

_____

_____

- *When you've tried to change before, what thoughts or feelings usually show up first? (Fear, doubt, shame, "this won't last," etc.)*

_____

_____

_____

_____

_____

_____

- *How does it feel to hear that resistance is normal and not a sign that you're broken?*

_____

_____

_____

_____

_____

Exercise: Familiar vs. Faithful Inventory

In each of the four sections (Faith, Health, Finances, Relationships), take a moment to reflect and fill in the two prompts inside each box:

FAITH

"Familiar Patterns I Tend to Fall Into"

"Faithful Patterns I Sense God Inviting Me Into"

HEALTH

"Familiar Patterns I Tend to Fall Into"

"Faithful Patterns I Sense God Inviting Me Into"

FINANCES

"Familiar Patterns I Tend to Fall Into"

"Faithful Patterns I Sense God Inviting Me Into"

RELATIONSHIPS

"Familiar Patterns I Tend to Fall Into"

"Faithful Patterns I Sense God Inviting Me Into"

Exercise: Familiar vs. Faithful Inventory Example

In each of the four sections (Faith, Health, Finances, Relationships), take a moment to reflect and fill in the two prompts inside each box:

FAITH

"Familiar Patterns I Tend to Fall Into"

Familiar: Scroll before bed, skip prayer, feel guilty.

"Faithful Patterns I Sense God Inviting Me Into"

Faithful: Read one Psalm before bed, say a 2-minute prayer, release the day to God.

HEALTH

"Familiar Patterns I Tend to Fall Into"

Familiar: Skip breakfast, live on coffee, crash mid-afternoon.

"Faithful Patterns I Sense God Inviting Me Into"

Faithful: Drink a glass of water in the morning, eat something with protein, take a short walk.

FINANCES

"Familiar Patterns I Tend to Fall Into"

Familiar: Avoid checking accounts, overspend when stressed.

"Faithful Patterns I Sense God Inviting Me Into"

Faithful: Weekly 10-minute money check-in with God, simple budget, one small step toward saving or giving.

RELATIONSHIPS

"Familiar Patterns I Tend to Fall Into"

Familiar: Stuff feelings, then explode or withdraw.

"Faithful Patterns I Sense God Inviting Me Into"

Faithful: Pray before hard conversations, speak truth with grace, set healthy boundaries.

You are not broken. You are being invited out of familiar patterns into faithful ones—with God's help, one small step at a time.

GRACE: *God Is Not Grading You*

Before you turn the page into more foundational work, we need to settle something: how you walk this journey matters just as much as what you do.

You will not do this perfectly. You will miss days. You will have weeks that feel messy. You will have moments where you want to quit.

That doesn't disqualify you.
It just makes you human.

This workbook is not about proving yourself to God. It's about walking with God as He gently reshapes your life.

> ### EPHESIANS 2:8–9
>
> *"For it is by grace you have been saved, through faith—and this is not from yourselves, it is the gift of God—not by works, so that no one can boast."*
>
> ### 2 CORINTHIANS 12:9
>
> *"But he said to me, 'My grace is sufficient for you, for my power is made perfect in weakness.'"*

Grace doesn't mean we don't try. It means we don't tie our worth to how perfectly we try. When you stumble, the question is not, "Why did I fail?"

The question is, "What can I learn, and how can I reengage again, always with grace?"

PACE: *You Don't Have to Rush*

You are a busy woman. You have limits. That's not a flaw; it's part of how God designed you.

This workbook is not asking you to overhaul your entire life in a week. It's inviting you to:

- Take one step at a time
- Make small, sustainable changes
- Honor the season you're in

If you need to move slowly, move slowly. If you need to pause and come back, pause and come back. The goal is not speed; the goal is faithfulness over time.

"

GALATIANS 6:9

"Let us not become weary in doing good, for at the proper time we will reap a harvest if we do not give up."

You can slow down.
You can pause and come back.
You can stay longer in a chapter that's really speaking to you.

Exercise: Defining Success Differently

If success is not "doing this perfectly," what is it?

"For this workbook, I will consider it a success if I…"

(Examples she might write:
"…show up consistently most weeks."
"…complete Part One."
"…take one real action in each area."
"…grow closer to God and hear His voice more clearly.")

_____

_____

_____

_____

_____

_____

_____

_____

_____

_____

_____

_____

_____

_____

WHEN YOU FALL OFF *(Because You Will)*

There will be days you don't open this. Weeks that feel off. Times you slip back into old patterns. That doesn't disqualify you, stop your progress, or in any way mean you have failed.

When that happens:
1. Notice it without shame.
2. Ask God what happened and what you need.
3. Pick one simple next step (re-read a section, answer one question, pray one honest prayer).

THE ENEMY SAYS:
"YOU BLEW IT. QUIT."

THE FATHER SAYS:
"YOU STUMBLED. TAKE MY HAND. LET'S KEEP WALKING."

How do you usually respond when you "fall off" a plan or habit?

_____

_____

_____

_____

_____

How do you usually respond when you "fall off" a plan or habit?

_____

_____

_____

_____

_____

TRANSITION INTO *the Rest of Part One*

As you move deeper into Part One: Foundations for Lasting Change, take a deep breath.
You don't have to fix your whole life in 7 days.

You're simply choosing to let God lead you through a powerful reset, and then keep walking with Him, one small step at a time, toward a life that reflects His peace, His wisdom, and His love in every area.

You have already done a lot on this journey! So far, you've:

- Acknowledged that change is hard—but you're not broken.
- Learned that your brain prefers familiar, but God is inviting you into faithful.
- Settled that this journey will be marked by grace, a sustainable pace, and real progress.

Now we're ready to go deeper into the foundations that will support lasting change:

- Renewing your mind with God's truth
- Rooting your identity in Christ
- Turning your intentions into integrated, sustainable habits

This is where your vision starts to move from idea to reality—with God, one step at a time.

IDENTITY-BASED TRANSFORMATION

Most of us try to change from the outside in:

"If I can just fix my habits, then I'll feel different. If I can just get it together, then I'll finally be the woman I'm supposed to be."

But in the Kingdom, transformation starts from the **inside out.**

God changes who you are on the inside (identity), which changes how you think (mindset), which then changes how you live (habits and actions). This chapter is about remembering who you are in Christ and learning to live **from** that identity, instead of striving to earn it.

WHO YOU ARE *in Christ*

Your roles can change. Your season can change. Your circumstances can change.

Your identity in Christ does not.

2 CORINTHIANS 5:17
"Therefore, if anyone is in Christ, the new creation has come: The old has gone, the new is here!"

EPHESIANS 1:3–4
"Praise be to the God and Father of our Lord Jesus Christ, who has blessed us in the heavenly realms with every spiritual blessing in Christ. For he chose us in him before the creation of the world to be holy and blameless in his sight."

1 PETER 2:9
"But you are a chosen people, a royal priesthood, a holy nation, God's special possession..."

Identity truths you can highlight on the page:

- I am loved.
- I am chosen.
- I am forgiven.
- I am God's workmanship.
- I am not defined by my past.
- I am a daughter of the King.

These truths are not rewards for good behavior. They are gifts of grace because of Jesus.

LIVING FROM IDENTITY, *Not for Identity*

Old way of thinking:

- "If I finally get healthy, then I'll be worthy."
- "If I get my finances together, then I'll be responsible."
- "If I fix my relationships, then I'll be lovable."
- "If I pray and read my Bible enough, then I'll be spiritual."

Kingdom way of thinking:

- "Because I am loved, I can honor my body."
- "Because I am a wise steward in Christ, I can learn new financial habits."
- "Because I am already loved and chosen, I can show up differently in relationships."
- "Because I am God's daughter, I desire to spend time with Him."

You are not working for an identity. You are working from the identity Jesus already paid for.

When you start with "who I am in Christ," your goals and habits become expressions of that identity—not attempts to earn it.

Exercise: Identity Inventory

This exercise helps you release old labels and embrace who God says you are.

Instructions:

In Column 1: Old Labels and Stories I've Carried, write the labels or beliefs you've held about yourself.

In Column 2: Who God Says I Am, write the truth from Scripture or identity statements that replace each old label.

When both columns are complete:
- Cross out the old labels in Column 1.
- Circle the truths in Column 2 as a prophetic act of agreeing with God's Word.

COLUMN 1 **OLD LABELS AND STORIES I'VE CARRIED** EXAMPLES: *"Too much"	"Not enough"	"Bad with money"* *"Lazy"	"Weak"	"Unlovable"	"Always a mess"*	COLUMN 2 **"WHO GOD SAYS I AM"** EXAMPLES: *Old: "I'm a mess."* *Truth: "I am a new creation in Christ." (2 Corinthians 5:17)*

Journaling Prompt

- *Which old identity labels have you worn for years? Where did they come from (family, culture, past experiences)?*

_____

_____

_____

_____

_____

_____

_____

_____

_____

- *How have those labels shaped your decisions in faith, health, finances, and relationships?*

_____

_____

_____

_____

_____

_____

_____

_____

_____

- Which identity truth from Scripture is hardest for you to believe right now? Why?

_____

_____

_____

_____

_____

_____

_____

_____

_____

_____

- If you fully embraced your identity in Christ, what would change first in your daily life?

_____

_____

_____

_____

_____

_____

_____

_____

_____

_____

Exercise: "I Am" Declarations

Write a page of "I am" statements rooted in Scripture, such as:

- I am a daughter of the King.
- I am clothed with strength and dignity. (Proverbs 31:25)
- I am created for such a time as this. (Esther 4:14)
- I am God's workmanship, created for good works. (Ephesians 2:10)
- I am not defined by my past; I am made new in Christ. (2 Corinthians 5:17)

When you're done, read your declarations out loud every day for the next 30 days as a practice of renewing your mind and strengthening your identity.

Write your own 'I am' declarations below. Speak them out loud as a reminder of who you already are in Christ.

_____

_____

_____

_____

_____

_____

_____

_____

_____

_____

_____

_____

_____

_____

IDENTITY-BASED *Goal Framework*

FOLLOW THE EXAMPLE BELOW AND COMPLETE THE NEXT PAGE.

Now we connect identity to action.
Instead of starting with "I want to..." start with:
"In Christ, I am a woman who..."

FAITH

Example:

Identity: "In Christ, I am a woman who walks closely with God."
Goal: "Because this is who I am, I will spend 10-15 minutes with God in Scripture and prayer 5 days a week for the next 90 days."
Habit: "I will read one chapter and write a short prayer at my kitchen table before I check my phone."

HEALTH

Example:

Identity: "In Christ, I am a woman who honors God with her body."
Goal: "Because this is who I am, I will walk for 20 minutes 4 days a week for the next 8 weeks."
Habit: "I will walk right after dinner on Monday, Wednesday, Friday, and Saturday."

FINANCES

Example:

Identity: "In Christ, I am a wise and generous steward."
Goal: "Because this is who I am, I will review my finances and create a simple budget by [date]."
Habit: "I will have a 15-minute money check-in with God every Sunday."

RELATIONSHIPS

Example:

Identity: "In Christ, I am a woman who loves others with truth and grace."
Goal: "Because this is who I am, I will initiate one brave, honest, loving conversation by [date]."
Habit: "I will pray for that person by name 3 times a week."

IDENTITY-BASED *Goal Framework*

Now we connect identity to action.
Instead of starting with "I want to..." start with:
"In Christ, I am a woman who..."

FAITH

HEALTH

FINANCES

RELATIONSHIPS

CLOSING THOUGHT:

Identity-based transformation means you are not trying to become someone else.
You are learning to live, think, and choose in agreement with who you already are in
Christ - one decision at a time.

GRACE OVER PERFECTION

As you begin to make changes, you will be tempted to fall back into old patterns of perfectionism and self-criticism:

"If I can't do it perfectly, why bother?"
"I missed a day; I've ruined it."
"Everyone else seems more disciplined than me."

This chapter is about choosing **grace over perfection** and learning how to keep going when you feel like you've "fallen off track."

PROGRESS, *Not Performance*

God is not impressed by your performance. He is moved by your trust and your willingness to walk with Him.

> ### EPHESIANS 2:8–9
> *"For it is by grace you have been saved, through faith—and this is not from yourselves, it is the gift of God—not by works, so that no one can boast."*
>
> ### GALATIANS 6:9
> *"Let us not become weary in doing good, for at the proper time we will reap a harvest if we do not give up."*
>
> ### LUKE 16:10
> *"Whoever can be trusted with very little can also be trusted with much..."*

Progress might look like:

- Choosing prayer over scrolling once today
- Drinking water instead of soda at one meal
- Checking your bank account instead of avoiding it
- Sending one text to reconnect or apologize
- Saying "no" once where you would have said "yes" out of guilt

These are not "small" to God. They are seeds of a new life.

Journaling Prompt

- *What does "progress" look like for you in this season, in each area (faith, health, finances, relationships)?*

_____

_____

_____

_____

_____

_____

- *How can you celebrate small wins instead of only noticing what's not done?*

_____

_____

_____

_____

_____

WHAT TO DO WHEN YOU *"Fall Off Track"*

You will have days, even weeks, where you don't follow your plan. That is normal.

The enemy's narrative:
"You blew it. You might as well quit."

The Father's heart:
"You stumbled. Take My hand. Let's keep walking."

When you feel like you've fallen off track:

1. Notice without shame.
- "I haven't opened this in a week."
- "I've been stress-eating again."
- "I ignored my budget this month."

2. Ask God what happened.
- Was I exhausted? Overcommitted? Triggered by something?
- What was I feeling? What did I need?

3. Receive grace.
- Remember: God's grace is not surprised by your humanity.
- His power is made perfect in weakness (2 Corinthians 12:9).

4. Choose one simple next step.
- Re-read one page that encouraged you.
- Answer one journaling question.

Take one small action aligned with your identity. (one prayer, one walk, one money check-in, one honest conversation).

Journaling Prompt

- *How do you usually respond when you "fall off" a plan or habit? (Be honest, sweet friend. It's just you and Jesus here.)*

_____

_____

_____

_____

_____

_____

_____

_____

- *What would a grace-filled, God-honoring response look like instead?*

_____

_____

_____

_____

_____

_____

_____

_____

_____

Exercise: Your Grace Plan, Defining Success Differently

Perfection defines success as "no mistakes, no missed days, no mess."

Grace defines success as "showing up, learning, and walking with God over time."

If success is not "doing this perfectly," what is it?

"For this workbook, I will consider it a success if I…"

Examples of you might write:
"…show up consistently most weeks."
"…complete Part One."
"…take one real action in each area."
"…grow closer to God and hear His voice more clearly."

_____

_____

_____

_____

_____

_____

_____

_____

_____

_____

_____

_____

_____

_____

Exercise: Your Grace Plan for When I Fall Off

Below I invite you to write:
One thing you will say to yourself (truth-based, kind, grounded in Scripture)
One prayer you will pray
One small action you can take within 24 hours

Example text you can write:
"When I notice I've fallen off track, instead of quitting, I will say to myself, 'I am still God's daughter, and He is not disappointed in me.' I will pray, 'Lord, thank You that Your grace is enough. Show me one small step to take today.' Then I will open this workbook and complete one question or one page."

"When I notice I've fallen off track, instead of quitting, I will..."

_____
_____
_____
_____
_____
_____
_____
_____
_____
_____
_____
_____
_____

CLOSING: *Moving Forward with Foundations*

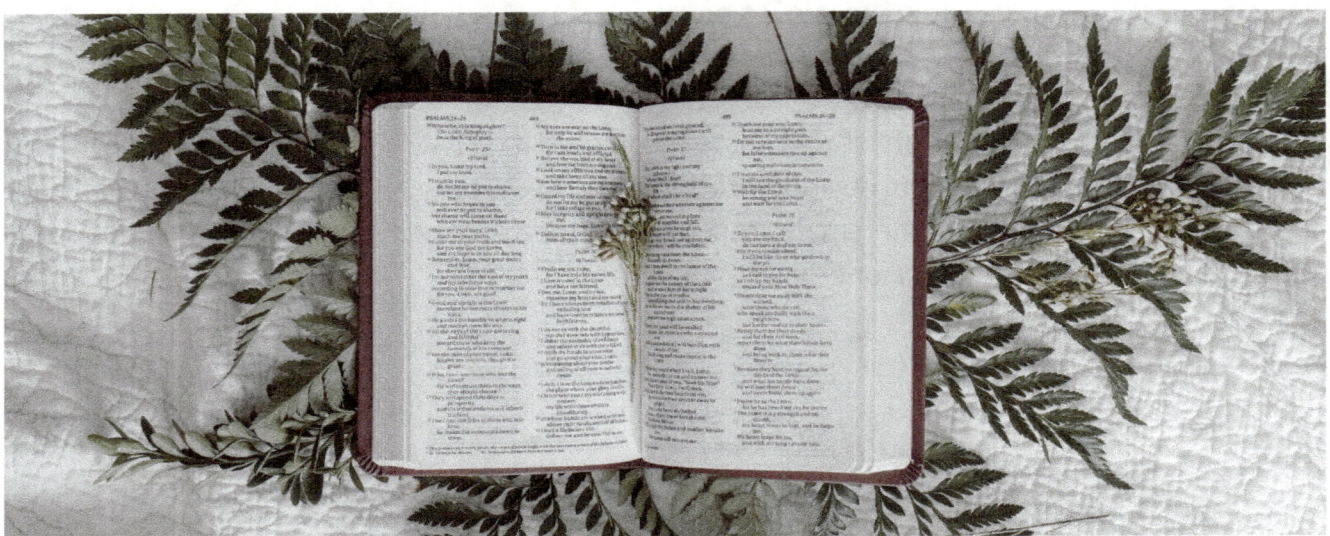

As you finish Part One: Foundations for Lasting Change, you have:

- A clearer understanding of why change feels hard (and why you're not broken)
- A deeper sense of who you are in Christ and how to live from that identity
- A commitment to grace over perfection, progress over performance

You are now ready to apply these foundations to your specific focus area—faith, health, finances, or relationships—and to walk out your 7-day reset and beyond with God.

This is not about fixing your whole life at once.

It's about walking with Jesus, one small, faithful step at a time, into the whole-life makeover He has in mind for you.

PART TWO:
Start Here – Your Assessment & Focus Area

In Part One, you built your foundations: you learned why change feels hard, anchored yourself in who you are in Christ, and chose grace over perfection.

Now it's time to get specific.

Part Two will help you:
- Understand your assessment results
- Choose your primary focus area for this season
- Make a clear, compassionate decision about where to start—especially if you feel like everything is "too much"

This is where your whole-life makeover becomes personal and practical.

Journaling Prompt

- *As you think about your real, everyday life right now, what feels most in need of God's touch—your faith, your health, your finances, your relationships, or your sense of purpose?*

_____

_____

_____

_____

_____

_____

_____

_____

_____

- *Why does that area matter so much to you in this season, and what are you hoping will be different as you walk through this process with Him?*

_____

_____

_____

_____

_____

_____

_____

_____

_____

UNDERSTANDING YOUR ASSESSMENT RESULTS

Your assessment is NOT a verdict on your worth. It IS a snapshot of your current season.

It's simply a tool to help you see:
- Where you're feeling the most pressure or pain
- Where a small shift could make a big difference
- Where God may be inviting you to focus first

Think of it as a conversation starter between you and the Holy Spirit.

WHAT YOUR *Results Reveal*

Your primary result will point you toward one of these profiles:

The Weary Warrior – Health & Wellness
You're carrying a lot, and your body, energy, or emotional health is paying the price. You may feel exhausted, burned out, or disconnected from your own needs.

The Hidden Heroine – Personal Development & Purpose
You sense there is more in you—gifts, dreams, calling—but you feel stuck, unclear, or unsure how to move forward. You've been cheering for everyone else and putting yourself last.

The Hungry Heart - Faith Life
You love God, but you feel spiritually dry, distracted, or distant. You want a deeper, more consistent connection with Him but struggle to find rhythm and focus.

The Stretched Steward – Finances

Money feels stressful, confusing, or heavy. You may be avoiding your numbers, living in survival mode, or unsure how to steward what you have with wisdom and peace.

The Pouring-From-Empty Giver – Relationships

You're always there for everyone else, but your relationships may feel one-sided, draining, or complicated. Boundaries are hard, and you're tired of feeling like you're giving from an empty cup.

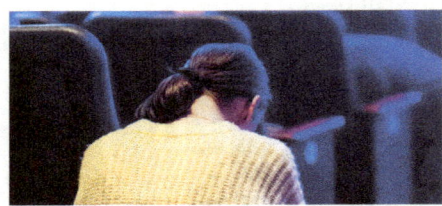

The Overloaded Overcomer – Whole-Life Overload

It feels like everything is on fire at once. You're juggling so much that it's hard to even know where to begin. You're not weak—you've just been in survival mode for a long time.

Your result doesn't label you; it highlights where you need the most care and attention in this season.

Journaling Prompt

- *How did you feel when you first saw your assessment result? (Relieved, surprised, defensive, seen, etc.)*

_____

_____

_____

_____

_____

_____

_____

_____

- *In what ways does your result feel accurate? In what ways did it challenge you?*

_____

_____

_____

_____

_____

_____

_____

_____

HOW TO READ YOUR SCORES

Your assessment may show:

- One clear primary profile (highest score)
- A strong primary profile with one or two close "secondary" areas
- A more even spread (often connected to the Overloaded Overcomer)

Use your scores to:

1. Identify your **primary focus** – the area that needs the most attention right now.
2. Notice your **secondary areas** – they matter too, but you don't have to fix everything at once.

What is your primary profile/result?

_____

_____

_____

_____

_____

_____

_____

_____

_____

_____

_____

What are your next highest areas?

_____
_____
_____
_____
_____
_____
_____
_____

As you look at your scores, what stands out to you the most?

_____
_____
_____
_____
_____
_____
_____
_____
_____

Please PLEASE remember this, sweet friend: Your scores are information, not condemnation. They are a starting point for healing, not a report card on your value.

CHOOSE YOUR PRIMARY FOCUS AREA

You might feel the urge to fix everything at the same time.

But trying to overhaul your entire life at once is the fastest way to burn out and quit. Real, sustainable change happens when you choose one primary focus area for this season and give yourself permission to start there.

You may even want to choose one primary focus area, and then drill down deeper into one sub-area that needs attention right now. This is a marathon, not a sprint, and we don't want to look at all the things all at once. This should not be another source of overwhelm, discontent, or self criticism. Many of the habits you have built over long periods of time are conspiring to defeat you all at once. Take the time to really correct one thing at a time and lean heavily on the Lord to make that happen. You can choose another area to focus on at another time. Deal?

THE FIVE KEY LIFE AREAS

For this workbook, we're focusing on five key areas that deeply affect your everyday life:

FAITH

Your relationship with God, spiritual rhythms, prayer, Scripture, and identity in Christ.

HEALTH

Your physical body, energy, rest, nutrition, movement, and emotional well-being.

FINANCES

Your money mindset, spending, saving, giving, debt, and stewardship.

RELATIONSHIPS

Your closest connections: family, friends, church, community, and boundaries.

PERSONAL DEVELOPMENT & PURPOSE

Your growth, gifts, calling, mindset, and sense of direction.

Weary Warrior → Health
(with emotional/spiritual
overlap)

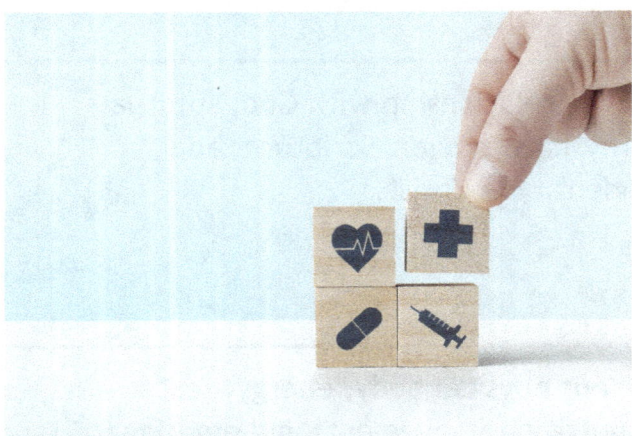

Hidden Heroine →
Personal Development
& Purpose

Hungry Heart →
Faith

Stretched Steward →
Finances

Pouring-From-Empty Giver
→ Relationships

Overloaded Overcomer
→ Needs triage
(we'll address this in Chapter 9)

Which area feels most painful, pressing, or unsustainable right now?

_____

_____

_____

_____

_____

Which area, if it started to heal or improve, would create the biggest ripple effect in the rest of your life?

_____

_____

_____

_____

_____

ONE AREA AT A TIME: *Why It Works*

Focusing on one primary area at a time:
- Reduces overwhelm
- Builds confidence and momentum
- Creates visible progress you can actually feel
- Often leads to natural improvements in other areas

Example:
- When you start sleeping better and moving your body (Health), your mood improves, you make clearer financial decisions, and you have more patience in relationships.
- When you get honest and intentional with your money (Finances), your stress decreases, which helps your health and your relationships.
- When you reconnect with God (Faith), you gain wisdom, peace, and direction that touches every area.

Based on your assessment and your own sense of what God is highlighting, which ONE area will you choose as your primary focus for the next 7 days (and beyond)?

"My primary focus area for this season is:

_____

Because_____

_____

_____

_____**"**

Note:

Choosing one area does not mean the others don't matter. It simply means you are choosing to be intentional and kind to yourself by starting where it counts most right now.

IF YOU'RE THE OVERLOADED OVERCOMER

Some women open this workbook and think, "I don't have just one problem. I have all of them."

If that's you, you're likely the Overloaded Overcomer.

You've been carrying a lot, for a long time. You've survived things other people don't even know about. You are strong, but you are tired.

This chapter is here to help you when everything feels like "too much" and you genuinely don't know where to start.

WHEN EVERYTHING *Feels Like Too Much*

When your whole life feels overwhelming, your brain often goes into:

- **Fight:** "I have to push harder and control everything."
- **Flight:** "If I stay busy enough or distracted enough, maybe I won't have to feel this."
- **Freeze:** "It's all too much. I can't deal with any of it."
- **Fawn:** "I'll just keep taking care of everyone else and ignore my own needs."
- **Flail:** "I'll try to fix everything at once for three days, then crash."

None of that means you're failing. It means your nervous system has been in survival mode.

Right now, the bravest thing you can do is not to fix everything. It's to choose one gentle, wise starting point.

And, since I'm encouraging radical honesty, I'll tell you this is where I started as well. Survival mode, exhaustion, discontent, fear, disconnect from the Father, overwhelm….you get it, and you're not alone.

Journaling Prompt

- When life feels like "too much," what do you usually do? (Shut down, over-function, numb out, overthink, etc.)

_____

_____

_____

_____

_____

_____

_____

_____

- How do you want to respond differently in this season?

_____

_____

_____

_____

_____

_____

_____

_____

HOW TO CHOOSE WHERE TO START

If you're the Overloaded Overcomer, use this simple triage approach:

Ask yourself three questions:

1. Where am I in the most immediate danger of burning out or breaking down?
    (This might point to Health or Relationships.)

2. Where am I feeling the loudest, constant stress or fear?
    (This might point to Finances, Health, or Relationships.)

3. Where do I sense God gently putting His finger right now?
    (This might surprise you—it could be Faith, or your sense of purpose, or a relationship.)

What are your honest answers to these three questions?

_____

_____

_____

_____

_____

_____

As you read them back, what area seems to be asking for attention first?

_____

_____

_____

_____

_____

SIMPLE STARTING FRAMEWORK FOR
Overloaded Overcomers

I am with you, sweet friend, and I have some suggestions if you are too overwhelmed to even decide where you're too overwhelmed. Choose one of the following very simple decision paths, and remember that we're just looking for a little bit of progress, which will lead to a little bit of momentum, which will lead (over time) to a lot of progress and a lot of momentum:

- If your body is exhausted, in pain, or constantly running on empty → **Start with Health.**
- If your soul feels spiritually dry, numb, or disconnected from God → **Start with Faith.**
- **If money stress is keeping you up at night → Start with Finances.**
- If you feel alone, resentful, or constantly people-pleasing → **Start with Relationships.**
- If you feel lost, directionless, or like you've disappeared inside your roles → **Start with Personal Development & Purpose.**

"Given everything I'm carrying, I will start here:

My first focus area will be_____

Because_____

_____

_____

_____**"**

PERMISSION TO START SMALL

If you're overloaded, your first goal might be very simple:
- Go to bed 30 minutes earlier three nights this week.
- Spend 5 minutes with God in the morning before you touch your phone.
- Look at your bank account once this week and talk to God about what you see.
- Send one text to a safe person and tell them you're tired and need prayer.

Small does not mean insignificant. It means **doable.**

You don't have to climb the whole mountain today.

You just have to take the next right step, in the right direction, with the One who climbs with you.

You are an overcomer who has been overloaded for a long time—and now, with God, you're choosing a kinder, wiser way forward.

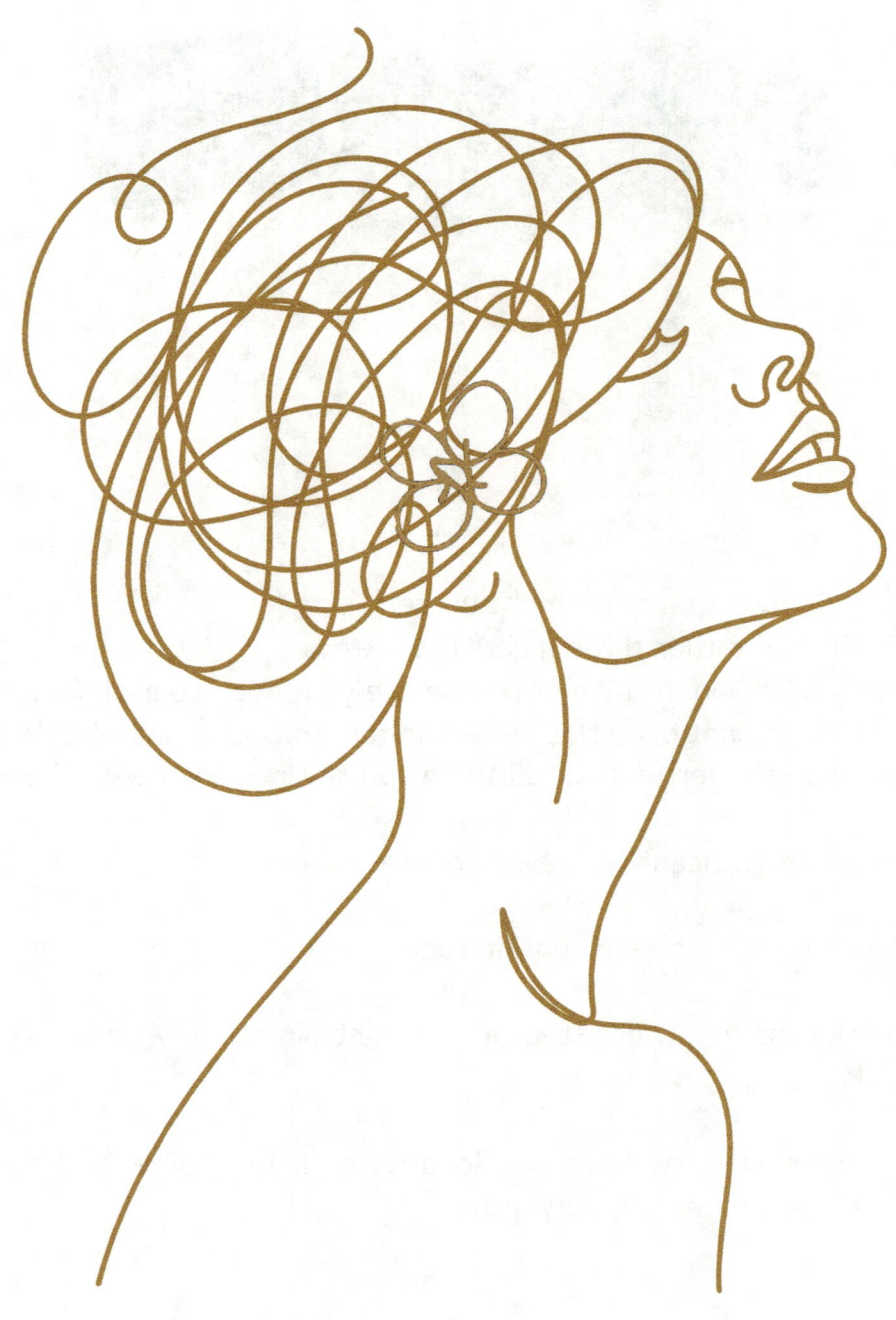

PART THREE:

Vision, Goals and habit with God at the center

You've laid your foundations and chosen your primary focus area.

Now it's time to:
- Picture where you're going with God
- Set gentle, doable goals
- Design simple habits and rhythms that fit your real life

This is where your whole-life makeover starts to show up in your calendar, your choices, and your everyday routines.

SUGGESTIONS ON HOW TO USE PART THREE + *Your Profile Guide*

Part Three gives you the **core framework** for change:
- Crafting a 90-day, God-centered vision
- Setting one main 90-day goal and monthly milestones
- Designing simple habits and daily rhythms

These pages are meant for **every woman**, no matter which profile you are.

Your **profile guide** (Weary Warrior, Hidden Heroine, Hungry Heart, Stretched Steward, or Pouring-From-Empty Giver) is where this framework gets **personal and specific**. In your guide, you'll find:
- Tailored encouragement for your season
- Honest check-in questions for your focus area
- Example 90-day goals and tiny habit ideas that fit your profile
- Weekly check-in prompts written just for you

How to use them together:
1. Use Part Three to:
    - Write your 90-day vision
    - Choose your main 90-day goal
    - Create your habit stacks and daily rhythm

2. Then turn to **your profile guide** to:
    - Refine your vision and goal with focus-area examples
    - Choose tiny habits from the menus that match your profile
    - Use the weekly check-ins to stay encouraged and on track

Think of Part Three as your **map**, and your profile guide as your **personalized route** for this season.

Prayer of Invitation

Holy Spirit, I invite You into this process.
I don't want to build my life on willpower,
pressure, or perfectionism.
I want to build it with You, in Your strength and
wisdom.

As I dream about the next 90 days, guide my
thoughts.
Show me what truly matters in this season.
Highlight the areas where You are already at
work,
and gently reveal the places You want to heal,
reorder, or strengthen.

Guard my heart from comparison and striving.
Help me set goals that are aligned with Your
heart for me—
not just what I think I "should" do.

Give me clarity, courage, and grace
to take small, faithful steps with You each day.
I surrender this process to You.
Lead me, Lord. Amen.

Journaling Prompt

As you sit with God and think about the next 90 days, what do you sense the Holy Spirit highlighting as most important for this season?

_____

_____

_____

_____

_____

_____

_____

_____

What do you feel Him inviting you toward (habits, healing, growth) and what do you feel Him inviting you to release (pressure, expectations, old patterns)?

_____

_____

_____

_____

_____

_____

_____

_____

CRAFTING A GOD-CENTERED VISION

Before you decide what to do, you need to see where you are going.

A God-centered vision is not a fantasy or a Pinterest board or an Instagram worthy photo. It's a prayerful picture of what your life could look like as you walk with God, one step at a time, for the next 90 days.

It's close enough to feel real and doable, but big enough to stretch your faith.

A PICTURE OF YOUR LIFE, *90 Days from Now*

"Imagine it's 90 days from today. You haven't done everything perfectly, but you have been walking with God and taking small, consistent steps in your focus area. Close your eyes and picture a regular day in your life."

Questions to guide your writing:

- What does your morning look and feel like?
- How do you feel in your body?
- How are you connecting with God throughout the day?
- How are you handling money decisions?
- What do your key relationships feel like—home, work, church, friendships?
- At the end of the day, what are you grateful for? What feels different from today?

My 90-Day God-Centered Vision

Faith

(MY WALK WITH GOD)

In 90 days, my relationship with God looks like...

_____

_____

_____

_____

Health

(BODY, ENERGY, EMOTIONS)

In 90 days, my health and energy look like...

_____

_____

_____

_____

Finances
(STEWARDSHIP & PEACE)

In 90 days, my finances look like...

_____

_____

_____

_____

_____

Relationships
(HOME, WORK, COMMUNITY)

In 90 days, my key relationships look like...

_____

_____

_____

_____

_____

Personal Development & Purpose

(IF THIS IS YOUR FOCUS)

In 90 days, my sense of purpose and growth looks like...

_____

_____

_____

_____

_____

"
"Lord, this is my vision with You at the center. Align my heart with Yours, and lead me step by step."

GENTLE, DOABLE GOAL SETTING

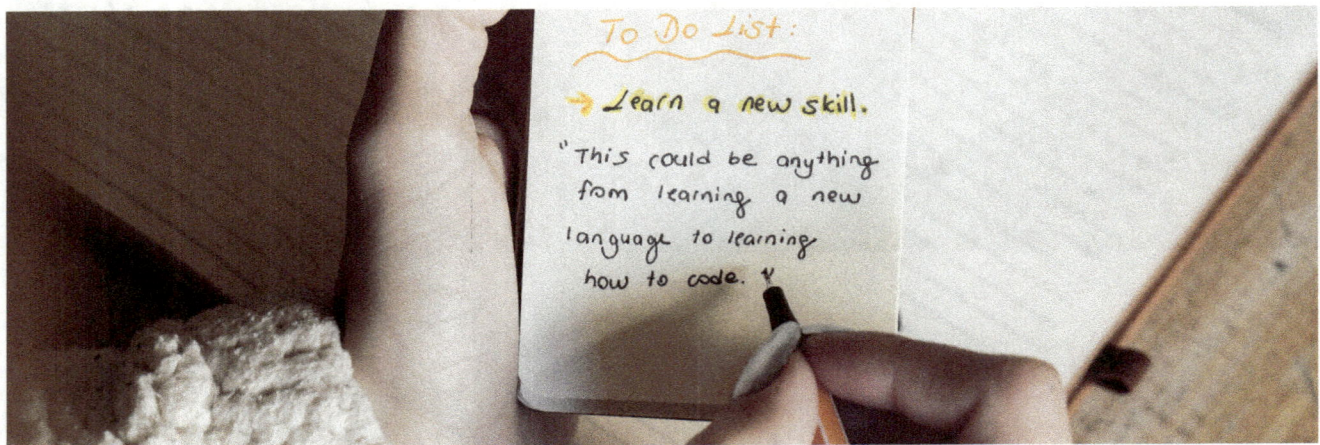

Now that you have a vision, it's time to choose one main goal for the next 90 days and break it down into smaller steps.

We're not creating a long to-do list. We're choosing a clear direction and a few simple markers along the way.

ONE MAIN *90 Day Goal*

Your main 90-day goal should:

- Align with your God-centered vision
- Be specific enough to measure
- Be gentle and realistic for your current season
- Focus on your primary area (faith, health, finances, relationships, or purpose)

Now that you've identified your 90-day vision and your primary focus area, it's time to create one clear 90-day goal.

This goal should be simple, specific, and aligned with the area you chose—not all five. Encourage yourself to choose the one thing that will create the greatest impact right now.

USE THE PROMPT BELOW TO WRITE YOUR GOAL IN THE NEXT PAGE:

"Based on my 90-day vision and my primary focus area, my main 90-day goal is..."

Here are some sample goals to guide your thinking:

- Faith: "Spend time with God in Scripture and prayer at least 5 days a week for the next 90 days."

- Health: "Walk for at least 20 minutes, 4 days a week, and be in bed by 10:30 p.m. most weeknights for the next 90 days."

- Finances: "Create and follow a simple monthly budget, track my spending weekly, and pay off $___ of debt in the next 90 days."

- Relationships: "Have one intentional, distraction-free connection (conversation, date, or quality time) each week with my spouse/child/friend for the next 90 days."

- Personal Development & Purpose: "Clarify my top 3 strengths and take one concrete step toward using them (class, project, or conversation) each month for the next 90 days."

Write just one main goal—the one that will move your life forward the most.

Journaling Prompt

Based on my 90-day vision and my primary focus area, my main 90-day goal is...

_____

_____

_____

_____

_____

_____

_____

_____

_____

_____

_____

_____

_____

_____

_____

_____

_____

_____

_____

MONTHLY MILESTONES
My 90-Day Goal & Monthly Milestones

Main 90-Day Goal:

_____

_____

_____

_____

Foundation
MONTH 1

By the end of Month 1, I will...
(Example: have a simple routine started, create a budget, schedule first counseling or coaching session, etc.)

_____

_____

_____

_____

_____

Consistency
MONTH 2

By the end of Month 2, I will...
(Example: be following my routine most weeks, have tracked spending for 4-8 weeks, have had 4 intentional connection times, etc.)

_____

_____

_____

_____

_____

Strengthening & Stretching
MONTH 3

By the end of Month 3, I will...
(Example: increase frequency or depth, pay off a specific amount, complete a project, have a key conversation, etc.)

_____

_____

_____

_____

_____

Journaling Prompt

- *What might try to get in the way of this 90-day goal (fear, schedule, other people's expectations, old habits)?*

_____

_____

_____

_____

_____

_____

_____

_____

- *How will you respond differently this time, with God's help?*

_____

_____

_____

_____

_____

_____

_____

_____

_____

HABIT STACKING & DAILY RHYTHMS

Big goals are reached through small, repeated actions.

Habits are how your vision and goals show up in your actual life—on Tuesday mornings, Thursday afternoons, and Saturday nights.

In this chapter, you'll learn how to use habit stacking and design simple daily rhythms that fit your season.

WHAT IS *Habit Stacking?*

Habit stacking is a simple way to build new habits by attaching them to habits you already do automatically.

Instead of trying to create a brand-new routine from scratch, you "stack" a new habit onto something that's already part of your day.

Now it's time to turn your 90-day goal into a simple daily or weekly rhythm using an "After I…, I will…" habit formula.

This helps you connect a new habit to something you already do, making it easier to stay consistent.

USE THE FORMULA BELOW TO WRITE YOUR HABIT:

Formula:

After I _____ (current habit), I will

_____(new habit).

HERE ARE SOME EXAMPLES TO SPARK IDEAS:

Faith:
- After I pour my morning coffee, I will read one Psalm and pray for 3 minutes.
- After I get into bed, I will write down one thing I'm grateful to God for.

Health:
- After I finish lunch, I will take a 10-minute walk.
- After I brush my teeth at night, I will fill my water bottle for tomorrow.

Finances:
- After I check my email in the evening, I will spend 5 minutes reviewing my spending for the day.
- After I get paid, I will immediately set aside my tithe and savings.

Relationships:
- After dinner on weeknights, I will put my phone away for 20 minutes and be fully present with my family.
- After church on Sunday, I will send one encouraging text to a friend or family member.

Choose one simple habit that supports your 90-day goal and write it using the formula above.

Habit stacking works because it uses your existing routines as anchors.

Habit Stack Form

Habits I Already Do Every Day	Possible New Habits to Stack
Examples	**Examples**
Wake up	Read one verse
Make coffee	Pray for 3 minutes
Check my phone	Drink a glass of water
Brush my teeth	Take a short walk
Eat lunch	Review my spending
Drive to work	Send an encouraging text
Put kids to bed	Stretch for 5 minutes
Watch TV in the evening	Write down 3 gratitudes
Get into bed	

In your primary focus area, what are 3-5 small habits that would support your 90-day goal?

_____

_____

_____

_____

_____

Use the formula below to write 4 habit Stacks:

HABIT 1:

After I _____,

I will _____.

HABIT 2:

After I _____,

I will _____.

HABIT 3:

After I _____,

I will _____.

HABIT 4:

After I _____,

I will _____.

DESIGNING YOUR
Daily Rhythm

Now, help her see how these habit stacks fit into a simple daily flow.
We're not building a rigid schedule; we're creating a gentle rhythm.

Morning Rhythm:

(Example: coffee + Scripture, short walk, gratitude list.)

"In the morning, my key habits will be…"

_____

_____

_____

_____

_____

Midday Rhythm:

(Example:lunch + 10-minute walk, water refill, brief prayer.)

"In the middle of the day, my key habits will be…"

_____

_____

_____

_____

_____

Evening Rhythm:

(Example: phone away during dinner, money check-in, 3-minute prayer before bed.)

"In the evening, my key habits will be…"

_____

_____

_____

_____

_____

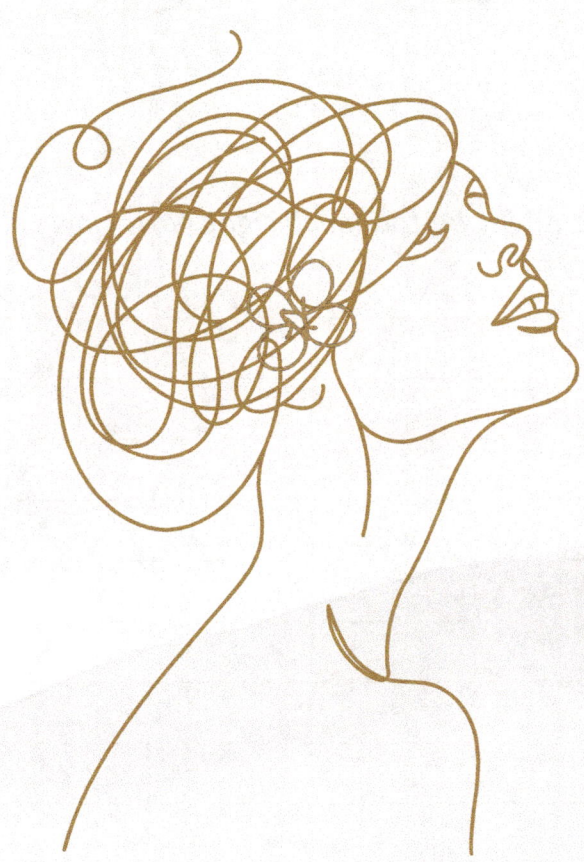

Journaling Prompt

- *Looking at your daily rhythm, what feels peaceful and doable?*

_____

_____

_____

_____

_____

_____

_____

- *What feels like it might be too much right now? How can you simplify it?*

_____

_____

_____

_____

_____

_____

_____

_____

Weekly Review & Reset

Sections:

"This week, I saw progress in..."

_____

_____

"This week was hard because..."

_____

_____

"What I learned about myself and my rhythms..."

_____

_____

"One small adjustment I will make next week..."

_____

_____

"My prayer for the week ahead..."

_____

_____

"

Vision gives you
direction.

Goals give you focus.

Habits & rhythms
give you a way to walk
it out—one ordinary
day at a time, with God
at the center.

PART FOUR:

Focus Area Guides

INTRODUCTION

By now, you've:
- Built a foundation of grace, identity, and renewed thinking
- Looked honestly at your whole life
- Chosen a primary focus area for this season
- Begun to craft a God-centered vision, goals, and habits

Now it's time to get even more personal.

Part Four is where your journey becomes tailored to what you're actually walking through. Each Focus Area Guide is designed to "meet you where you are" and help you apply everything you've learned to one specific part of your life.

In this section, you'll find guides for:
- The Weary Warrior – Health & Wellness
- The Hidden Heroine – Personal Development & Purpose
- The Hungry Heart – Faith Life
- The Stretched Steward – Finances
- The Pouring-From-Empty Giver – Relationships

Each guide follows a similar flow:
1. **Encouragement for Your Season**
   - A short word to remind you that you're seen, not judged—and that God is already at work.
2. **Honest Check-In**
   - Gentle questions to help you tell the truth about where you are right now in this area.
3. **Tiny Shifts, Big Impact**
   - A menu of small, doable habit ideas that fit your focus area and your real life.
4. **Choose Your Focus**
   - Space to set a simple 90-day goal and 1-3 habit stacks that support it.
5. **Weekly Check-In Pages**
   - A rhythm for reflecting, adjusting, and noticing how God is moving over time.

You do **not** need to complete every guide right now.

Start with the guide that matches your primary focus area (the profile you identified earlier). You can always come back to the others in future seasons as God leads.

As you move into these pages, remember:
You are not trying to become a different woman.
You are learning to live more fully as the woman God already says you are—
in your body, your mind, your money, your relationships, and your purpose.

Next, find your specific section and let's get to work!

SECTION A:
The Weary Warrior – Health and Wellness

as a primary pain point—or if you simply know in your heart:

"I am tired. My body, my energy, or my emotions are not okay, and I can't keep living like this."

This guide will help you invite God into your health in a gentle, sustainable way—no shame, no extremes, no "all or nothing."

Encouragement for the Weary Warrior

You are not weak because you're tired.

You are not lazy because you're worn out.

You are not failing because your body is asking for help.

You have been carrying a lot for a long time.

God sees every late night, every early morning, every hidden sacrifice, every time you pushed through when you were already empty.

Your body is not your enemy. It is a gift and a temple of the Holy Spirit.

1 CORINTHIANS 6:19–20
"Do you not know that your bodies are temples of the Holy Spirit, who is in you, whom you have received from God? You are not your own; you were bought at a price. Therefore honor God with your bodies."

3 JOHN 1:2
"Dear friend, I pray that you may enjoy good health and that all may go well with you, even as your soul is getting along well."

This section is not about chasing a certain size or "fixing" your body. It's about:
- Listening to what your body has been trying to tell you
- Honoring your limits instead of resenting them
- Making small, kind choices that support the life God is calling you to live

You are a weary warrior - but you are still a warrior. And God cares deeply about your rest, your health, and your strength.

Journaling Prompt

- *In your own words, how would you describe your relationship with your body and your energy right now?*

_____

_____

_____

_____

_____

- *What do you sense God might want to say to you about your health in this season?*

_____

_____

_____

_____

_____

HONEST CHECK-IN:
Your Body and Energy Today

This is your moment to tell the truth—with compassion, not criticism.

RATE EACH FROM 1-10 (1 = VERY POOR, 10 = EXCELLENT):

Energy during the day: _____

Sleep quality: _____

Movement/physical activity: _____

Nourishment (how you eat and hydrate): _____

Stress level (1 = calm, 10 = maxed out): _____

- *When do you feel most drained during the day? (Morning, afternoon, evening?)*

  _____

  _____

  _____

- *What are your top 1–2 "energy leaks" right now? (Examples: staying up late scrolling, skipping meals, constant stress, no breaks, saying yes to too much.)*

  _____

  _____

  _____

- *What is one thing your body has been trying to tell you that you've been ignoring?*

  _____

  _____

  _____

TINY SHIFTS, BIG IMPACT:
Health Habit Ideas

You do **not** need a massive overhaul.

You need a few **tiny, kind shifts** that you can actually sustain.

Use this as a **menu**, not a to-do list. Circle or highlight the ones that feel realistic for you in this season.

FAITH + HEALTH (BODY & SOUL TOGETHER)
- Pray a simple "Lord, strengthen me" prayer while you stretch for 3-5 minutes.
- Read one verse and take 5 deep breaths before bed.
- Listen to worship music during a short walk.

SLEEP & REST
- Set a "start winding down" alarm 30-60 minutes before bed.
- Charge your phone outside your bed or across the room.
- Create a 5-minute bedtime routine (wash face, stretch, gratitude, prayer).

MOVEMENT
- Take a 10-minute walk after lunch or dinner.
- Do a 5-minute stretch when you wake up.
- Walk while you're on a phone call (if possible).

NOURISHMENT
- Drink a glass of water first thing in the morning.
- Add one serving of fruit or vegetables to one meal each day.
- Pack a simple snack so you're not skipping meals.

STRESS & OVERWHELM

- Pause for 3 deep breaths + "Jesus, be my peace" before responding to stress.
- Take a 5-minute "no phone" break in the afternoon.
- Use a 15-minute "reset" block to tidy, plan, or step outside instead of spiraling.

Choose Your Health Focus

Now we'll bring Part Three's framework into your health focus as a Weary Warrior.

"In the middle of the day, my key habits will be…"

_____

_____

_____

_____

_____

Examples:
"Walk for at least 20 minutes, 4 days a week, for the next 90 days."
"Be in bed with screens off by 10:30 p.m. at least 5 nights a week."
"Eat 3 actual meals most days and drink at least 64 oz of water daily."
"Schedule and attend all needed medical/health appointments in the next 90 days."

MONTHLY MILESTONES
My 90-Day Goal & Monthly Milestones

MONTH 1

By the end of Month 1, I will...
(Example: establish a basic bedtime, start walking 2-3x/week.)

_____

_____

_____

_____

MONTH 2

By the end of Month 2, I will...
(Example: be walking 4x/week most weeks, consistently drinking more water.)

_____

_____

_____

_____

MONTH 3

By the end of Month 3, I will...
(Example: feel a noticeable shift in energy, have kept my main habit most weeks.)

_____

_____

_____

_____

1-3 HEALTH HABIT STACKS

Use the formula below to write 4 habit Stacks:

HABIT 1:

After I _____,

I will _____.

HABIT 2:

After I _____,

I will _____.

HABIT 3:

After I _____,

I will _____.

Examples:
After I pour my morning coffee, I will drink a full glass of water.
After I eat lunch, I will walk for 10 minutes.
After I put my phone on the charger at night, I will stretch for 3 minutes and pray.
After I finish work (or the kids' bedtime), I will sit for 2 minutes, breathe deeply, and ask God, "How am I really doing?"

Journaling Prompt

- *How do these small habits support the woman you are becoming in Christ—physically, emotionally, and spiritually?*

Weary Warrior Weekly Check-In

Sections:

"This Week, I Honored My Body By..."

(Space to list 3–5 ways she cared for her health, even small ones.)

_____

_____

"This Week Was Hard Because..."

(Space to be honest about stress, setbacks, or challenges.)

_____

_____

"I Noticed My Energy Was Better When..."

(Space to reflect on what actually helped.)

_____

_____

"One Small Adjustment I Will Make Next Week Is..."

(Space for a simple tweak—earlier bedtime, shorter walks, more water, etc.)

_____

_____

"My Prayer for My Body & Health This Week..."

(Space to write a short prayer.)

_____

_____

You don't have to become a different woman to be healthy.
You are already a beloved daughter of God, learning to care for the body He gave you—one gentle choice at a time.

SECTION B:
The Hidden Heroine – Personal Development & Purpose

This section is for you if your assessment highlighted **personal development & purpose** as a primary need—or if you quietly know:

"There is more in me than what I'm currently living. I feel hidden, stuck, or unsure how to move forward in who God made me to be."

This guide will help you reconnect with your God-given identity, gifts, and direction in a way that is gentle, practical, and rooted in truth.

Encouragement for the Hidden Heroine

You have a sense that you were made for more—but "more" has felt confusing, delayed, or out of reach.

Maybe you've spent years:
- Cheering for everyone else while putting yourself last
- Carrying roles and responsibilities that leave little room for your own growth
- Feeling like your gifts are sitting on the shelf, unused or unnoticed

You are not behind. You are not "too late." You are not disqualified.
You are a heroine in God's story—even if you feel hidden right now.

EPHESIANS 2:10
"For we are God's workmanship, created in Christ Jesus to do good works, which God prepared in advance for us to do."

ESTHER 4:14
"...And who knows but that you have come to your royal position for such a time as this?"

Your purpose is not a job title or a platform. It's a way of partnering with God to love, serve, and build in the places He's assigned to you.

Journaling Prompt

- *Where do you feel "hidden" right now—in your gifts, your calling, or your desires?*

_____

_____

_____

_____

_____

_____

_____

- *If you could say it without fear, what do you secretly wish you could do or become in this season?*

_____

_____

_____

_____

_____

_____

_____

HONEST CHECK-IN:
Your Growth and Purpose Today

This is your space to tell the truth about how you feel in this area—without judgment.

RATE EACH FROM 1-10 (1 = VERY POOR, 10 = EXCELLENT):

Clarity about my gifts and strengths: ____

Sense of direction or purpose in this season: ____

Time/space for my own growth (learning, dreaming, planning): ____

Confidence in using my voice and gifts: ____

Alignment between my daily life and what I feel called to: ____

- *Where in your life do you feel most "alive" or energized right now?*

  _____

  _____

  _____

- *Where do you feel most drained, bored, or stuck?*

  _____

  _____

  _____

- *What have you put on the back burner "until later" when it comes to your growth or calling?*

  _____

  _____

  _____

TINY SHIFTS, BIG IMPACT:
Growth & Purpose Habits

You don't need to overhaul your entire life or quit everything to "find your purpose."

You need a few **tiny, intentional shifts** that create space for clarity, learning, and obedience.

Use this as a **menu**, not a checklist. Circle or highlight what fits your season.

FAITH + PURPOSE
- Ask God each morning: "Lord, how do You want to use me today?"
- Read one passage about calling/obedience (e.g., Esther, Nehemiah, Proverbs 31, Ephesians 2) once a week.
- Spend 5 minutes journaling after church about what stood out and how you might apply it.

CLARITY & REFLECTION
- 10-minute weekly "brain dump" of ideas, dreams, and things that light you up.
- Once a week, answer: "What gave me life this week? What drained me?"
- List 3 things you're good at or people often thank you for.

LEARNING & SKILL-BUILDING
- Read 10 pages of a book related to your interests or calling, 3x/week.
- Listen to one podcast/teaching a week on a topic you want to grow in.
- Take one small, low-pressure class, workshop, or training over the next 90 days.

COURAGE & ACTION

- Share one idea or insight with a trusted friend each week.
- Say "yes" to one small opportunity to serve or lead in your church, community, or work.
- Practice using your voice once a week (speaking up in a meeting, sharing a thought, posting something meaningful).

BOUNDARIES & SPACE

- Block 30-60 minutes once a week as "growth time" (reading, planning, dreaming).
- Say "no" to one non-essential commitment this month to protect your energy.
- Turn off notifications for one hour a day to think and be present.

Which 2–4 tiny habits from this list feel most realistic and exciting for you right now?

_____

_____

_____

_____

_____

_____

_____

_____

_____

Choose Your Growth and Purpose Focus

Now we'll bring Part Three's framework into your Hidden Heroine focus.

*"Based on my honest check-in and my 90-day vision, my **one main 90-day growth/purpose goal** is..."*

_____

_____

_____

_____

_____

Examples:
"Clarify my top 3 strengths and intentionally use them each week for the next 90 days."
"Finish one book or course related to my interests/calling in the next 90 days."
"Spend 30 minutes once a week planning, reflecting, and praying over my calling."
"Say yes to one specific opportunity to serve/lead and show up faithfully for the next 90 days."

MONTHLY MILESTONES

My 90-Day Goal & Monthly Milestones

MONTH 1

By the end of Month 1, I will...

(Example: identify my top strengths, choose a book or course, block weekly growth time.)

_____

_____

_____

_____

MONTH 2

By the end of Month 2, I will...

(Example: be halfway through my book/course, have used my strengths intentionally several times.)

_____

_____

_____

_____

MONTH 3

By the end of Month 3, I will...

(Example: complete the book/course, have taken one concrete step in line with my calling.)

_____

_____

_____

1-3 GROWTH & PURPOSE HABIT STACKS

Use the formula below to write habit Stacks:

HABIT 1:

After I _____,

I will _____.

HABIT 2:

After I _____,

I will _____.

HABIT 3:

After I _____,

I will _____.

Examples (she can copy or adapt):

After I put my kids to bed, I will spend 10 minutes reading something that grows me.
After church on Sunday, I will write down one takeaway and one possible action step.
After I finish my morning coffee, I will ask God, "How do You want to use me today?"
After I sit down at my desk, I will review my top 3 priorities for the day.

Journaling Prompt

- *How do these small habits support the woman you already are in Christ—and the story you believe He's writing with your life?*

_____

_____

_____

_____

_____

_____

_____

_____

_____

_____

_____

_____

_____

_____

_____

_____

_____

Growth and Purpose Weekly Check-In

Sections:

This Week, I Invested in My Growth By...

(Space to list 3–5 ways she learned, reflected, or took action.)

_____

_____

This Week Was Hard Because...

(Space to be honest about resistance, fear, or obstacles.)

_____

_____

I Felt Most Alive or "On Purpose" When...

(Space to notice what activities, conversations, or moments lit her up.)

_____

_____

One Small Step I Will Take Next Week Is...

(Space for a simple, concrete action—send an email, finish a chapter, schedule a conversation, say yes/no.)

_____

_____

My Prayer for My Growth & Calling This Week...

(Space to write a short prayer.)

_____

_____

*You don't have to have your whole calling figured out to walk in purpose.
You are a hidden heroine, taking small, faithful steps with God—
and He knows exactly how to bring you into the right rooms, at the right
time, for the right reasons.*

SECTION C:
The Hungry Heart - Faith Life

This section is for you if your assessment highlighted faith life as a primary need—or if, deep down, you know:

"I love God, but I feel spiritually dry, distracted, or distant. I want a deeper, more consistent connection with Him."

This guide will help you reconnect with God in a way that is simple, honest, and sustainable—no spiritual performance, no guilt trips, just real relationship.

Encouragement for the Hungry Heart

You love Jesus—but lately, it may feel like:
- Your time with God is inconsistent or almost non-existent
- You're going through the motions at church but feel numb inside
- You're easily distracted when you try to pray or read Scripture
- You miss the closeness you once felt with God, or wish you'd ever felt it at all

If that's you, hear this clearly:
A hungry heart is not a failing heart.
A hungry heart is a **living** heart.
Your desire for more of God is evidence that He is already drawing you.

JAMES 4:8
"Come near to God and he will come near to you."

PSALM 63:1
"You, God, are my God, earnestly I seek you;
I thirst for you, my whole being longs for you,
in a dry and parched land where there is no water."

MATTHEW 5:6

"Blessed are those who hunger and thirst for righteousness, for they will be filled."

God is not rolling His eyes at your inconsistency. He is delighted that you want Him. He is ready to meet you in small, simple moments of honesty and attention.

Journaling Prompt

- *How would you honestly describe your relationship with God in this season—using your own words?*

_____

_____

_____

_____

_____

_____

_____

- *When in your life have you felt closest to God? What was different about that time?*

_____

_____

_____

_____

_____

_____

_____

HONEST CHECK-IN:
Your Faith Life Today

This is a safe place to tell the truth about where you are spiritually—without shame.

RATE EACH FROM 1-10 (1 = VERY POOR, 10 = EXCELLENT):

Sense of closeness with God: _____

Consistency in time with God (Bible, prayer, worship): _____

Ability to hear God's voice or sense His leading: _____

Engagement at church/community (present vs. just attending): _____

Alignment between what you believe and how you actually live: _____

- *What makes it hardest for you to spend time with God right now?*
  (Time, distraction, guilt, not knowing what to do, spiritual dryness, etc.)

  _____

  _____

  _____

- *When you think about approaching God, what feelings come up first?*
  (Joy, fear, shame, indifference, longing, confusion?)

  _____

  _____

  _____

- *What do you wish your relationship with God could look like in this season?*

  _____

  _____

  _____

Journaling Prompt

- *If you could say one completely honest sentence to God about where you are right now, what would it be?*

_____

_____

_____

_____

_____

_____

_____

_____

_____

_____

_____

_____

_____

_____

_____

_____

_____

_____

_____

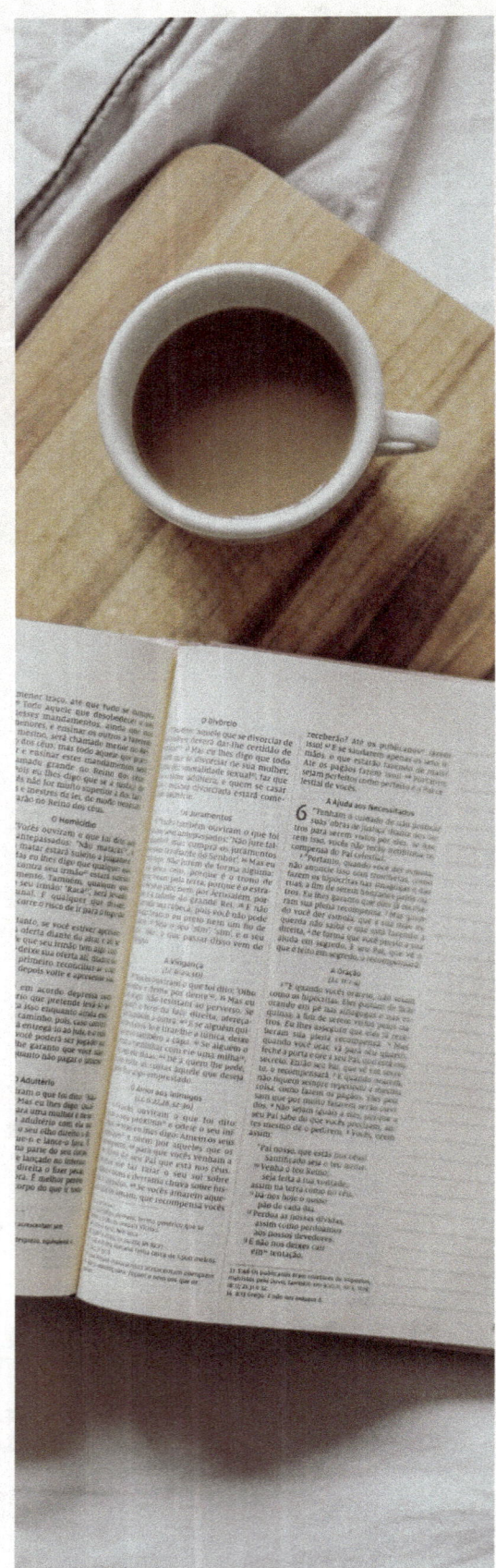

TINY SHIFTS, BIG IMPACT:
Faith Habit Ideas

You don't need a 2-hour quiet time to have a real relationship with God.

You need **small, consistent moments** of turning your attention toward Him.

Use this as a **menu**, not a checklist. Circle or highlight what fits your season.

SCRIPTURE

- Read one Psalm or one Proverb a day.
- Read one chapter from the Gospels (Matthew, Mark, Luke, John) 3x/week.
- Choose one verse for the week and write it where you'll see it often.

PRAYER

- Pray for 3 minutes in the morning before you touch your phone.
- Pray one simple breath prayer throughout the day, such as:
  - "Jesus, be my peace."
  - "Lord, lead me."
  - "Holy Spirit, help me."
- Keep a short "prayer list" and pray for one person each day.

WORSHIP & PRESENCE

- Play worship music while you get ready or drive.
- Take a 5-minute "presence pause" once a day— no phone, just breathing and inviting God into your moment.
- At the end of the day, thank God for 3 specific things.

COMMUNITY & ACCOUNTABILITY

- Text one friend each week and ask, "How can I pray for you?"
- Join or re-engage with a small group, Bible study, or church gathering.
- Ask a trusted friend to check in with you about your faith habits once a week.

OBEDIENCE & APPLICATION

- After church or a sermon, write down one thing you sense God asking you to do, not just think about.
- Take one small step of obedience each week (forgive, encourage, give, apologize, serve).

Which 2–4 tiny faith habits from this list feel most realistic and life-giving for you right now?

_____

_____

_____

_____

_____

_____

_____

_____

Choose Your Faith Focus

Now we'll bring Part Three's framework into your Hungry Heart focus.

*Based on my honest check-in and my 90-day vision, my **one main 90-day faith goal** is…*

_____

_____

_____

_____

_____

Examples:
"Spend time with God in Scripture and prayer at least 5 days a week for the next 90 days."
"Read through the Gospel of John and journal once a week about what I'm learning."
"Rebuild my connection with my church by attending weekly and joining one group or team in the next 90 days."
"Practice a daily gratitude + prayer routine before bed for the next 90 days."

MONTHLY MILESTONES
My 90-Day Goal & Monthly Milestones

MONTH 1
By the end of Month 1, I will...
(Example: establish a simple daily or 3x/week rhythm, choose a reading plan.)

_____

_____

_____

_____

MONTH 2
By the end of Month 2, I will...
(Example: have completed a certain number of chapters, feel more comfortable talking to God honestly.)

_____

_____

_____

_____

MONTH 3
By the end of Month 3, I will...
(Example: see a noticeable shift in my sense of closeness with God and my consistency.)

_____

_____

_____

_____

1-3 FAITH HABIT STACKS

Use the formula below to write habit Stacks:

HABIT 1:

After I _____,

I will _____.

HABIT 2:

After I _____,

I will _____.

HABIT 3:

After I _____,

I will _____.

Examples (she can copy or adapt):
After I pour my morning coffee, I will read one Psalm and pray for 3 minutes.
After I get into bed, I will write down one thing I'm grateful to God for.
After I finish dinner, I will take 5 minutes to step outside and talk to God about my day.
After church on Sunday, I will write one takeaway and one action step.

Journaling Prompt

- *How do these simple habits reflect the kind of relationship with God you truly desire?*

_____

_____

_____

_____

_____

_____

_____

_____

_____

_____

_____

_____

_____

_____

_____

_____

_____

_____

Hungry Heart Weekly Check-In

Sections:

This Week, I Connected with God By...
(Space to list 3–5 ways she prayed, read, worshiped, or noticed God.)

_____

_____

This Week Was Hard Spiritually Because...
(Space to be honest about distraction, doubt, dryness, or resistance.)

_____

_____

I Felt Closest to God When...
(Space to reflect on moments of peace, conviction, comfort, or joy.)

_____

_____

One Small Step I Will Take Next Week Is...
(Space for a simple action—set an alarm, choose a reading plan, attend church, text a friend.)

_____

_____

My Prayer for My Faith This Week...
(Space to write a short, honest prayer.)

_____

_____

God is not asking you for perfection.
He is inviting you into a real, living relationship—
one honest conversation, one small moment of attention, one step of
obedience at a time.

SECTION D:
The Stretched Steward — Finances

This section is for you if your assessment highlighted finances as a primary pain point—or if you know:

"Money feels heavy, stressful, or confusing. I want to handle it with wisdom and peace, not fear and avoidance."

This guide will help you face your finances with God—not in shame, but in stewardship, clarity, and small, doable steps.

Encouragement for the Stretched Steward

Money can stir up a lot of emotions:
- Anxiety when you look at your accounts (or avoid looking)
- Guilt over past decisions or current debt
- Shame that you "should be further along by now"
- Confusion about where it all goes and how to get ahead

If that's you, hear this:
You are not "bad with money" by identity.
You are a daughter of God learning to steward what He's entrusted to you.

God cares about your finances not because He's obsessed with numbers, but because:
- Money affects your peace
- Money affects your relationships
- Money affects your ability to give, serve, and build with Him

JAMES 1:5

"If any of you lacks wisdom, you should ask God, who gives generously to all without finding fault, and it will be given to you."

LUKE 16:10

"Whoever can be trusted with very little can also be trusted with much..."

PHILIPPIANS 4:19

"And my God will meet all your needs according to the riches of his glory in Christ Jesus."

You are not alone in this. God is willing to walk with you through every spreadsheet, every bill, every payment, every decision.

- *How would you honestly describe your relationship with God in this season—using your own words?*

_____

_____

_____

_____

- *When in your life have you felt closest to God? What was different about that time?*

_____

_____

_____

_____

_____

HONEST CHECK-IN:
Your Money Reality Today

This is your moment to tell the truth about where you are financially—without beating yourself up.

RATE EACH FROM 1-10 (1 = VERY POOR, 10 = EXCELLENT):

Clarity about my current financial situation: _____

Confidence in managing money (spending, saving, giving): _____

Consistency in tracking or checking my finances: _____

Peace level around money (vs. anxiety): _____

Alignment between my money habits and my values/faith: _____

- *How often do you currently look at your bank accounts or budget?*

  _____
  _____
  _____

- *Where do you feel most "out of control" with money? (Spending, debt, irregular income, emergencies, etc.)*

  _____
  _____
  _____

- *Where do you feel you're already doing something wise or faithful with money, even if it's small?*

  _____
  _____
  _____

Journaling Prompt

- If your finances could talk, what would they say about how they're being treated?

_____

_____

_____

_____

_____

_____

_____

_____

_____

_____

_____

_____

_____

_____

_____

_____

_____

_____

TINY SHIFTS, BIG IMPACT:
Money Habit Ideas

You don't need a complicated financial system to start stewarding well.

You need a few tiny, consistent habits that help you see clearly and act wisely.

Use this as a menu. Circle or highlight what fits your season.

AWARENESS & CLARITY

- Check your main bank account(s) once a day or a few times a week.
- Do a 10-15 minute "Money Monday" or "Finance Friday" check-in each week.
- List all your debts and bills in one place (even if it's uncomfortable).

SPENDING

- Track your spending for 7-30 days (app, notebook, or spreadsheet).
- Set a simple "spending pause" rule (wait 24 hours before non-essential purchases).
- Choose one spending category to gently reduce this month (e.g., eating out, impulse online buys).

SAVING & PLANNING

- Set up an automatic transfer of even a small amount to savings each pay period.
- Start a simple emergency fund (even $10-20 at a time).
- Create a basic monthly budget with just a few main categories.

GIVING & GENEROSITY

- Pray: "Lord, how do You want me to give in this season?"
- Start or re-start regular giving (tithe or a set percentage/amount).
- Choose one person, family, or ministry to bless in a small, intentional way this month.

MINDSET & PRAYER

- When you feel money anxiety, pray: "Lord, You are my Provider. Show me the next wise step."
- Replace "I'm terrible with money" with "I am learning to steward money with God's wisdom."
- Read one Scripture about God's provision or stewardship each week.

Which 2–4 tiny money habits from this list feel most realistic and helpful for you right now?

_____

_____

_____

_____

_____

_____

_____

_____

Choose Your Financial Focus

Now we'll bring Part Three's framework into your Stretched Steward focus.

*Based on my honest check-in and my 90-day vision, my **one main 90-day financial goal** is...*

_____

_____

_____

_____

_____

Examples:
"Create and follow a simple monthly budget for the next 3 months."
"Track all my spending for the next 90 days."
"Pay off $_____ of debt in the next 90 days."
"Build an emergency fund of $_____ in the next 90 days."
"Re-establish consistent giving (tithing or a set amount) for the next 90 days."

MONTHLY MILESTONES
My 90-Day Goal & Monthly Milestones

MONTH 1
By the end of Month 1, I will...
(Example: know all my balances, create a basic budget, track spending.)

_____

_____

_____

_____

MONTH 2
By the end of Month 2, I will...
(Example: have followed my budget most weeks, paid down some debt or added to savings.)

_____

_____

_____

_____

MONTH 3
By the end of Month 3, I will...
(Example: see a clear shift in my awareness, peace, and progress toward my goal.)

_____

_____

_____

_____

1-3 MONEY HABIT STACKS

Use the formula below to write 4 habit Stacks:

HABIT 1:

After I _____,

I will _____.

HABIT 2:

After I _____,

I will _____.

HABIT 3:

After I _____,

I will _____.

Examples (she can copy or adapt):

After I check my email in the evening, I will spend 5 minutes reviewing my spending for the day.

After I get paid, I will immediately set aside my tithe and savings before spending anything else.

After dinner on Sunday, I will do a 15-minute "Money Check-In" for the week ahead.

After I open my banking app, I will pray, "Lord, thank You for what I have. Show me how to steward it."

Journaling Prompt

- *How do these small habits move you toward being the wise, peaceful steward you believe God is calling you to be?*

_____

_____

_____

_____

_____

_____

_____

_____

_____

_____

_____

_____

_____

_____

_____

_____

_____

_____

_____

_____

Stretched Steward Weekly Check-In

Sections:

This Week, I Faced My Finances By...

(Space to list 3–5 ways she checked in, tracked, planned, or made a wise choice.)

_____

_____

This Week Was Hard Financially Because...

(Space to be honest about unexpected expenses, temptations, emotions, or setbacks.)

_____

_____

A Win (Even a Small One) From This Week Was...

(Space to celebrate progress—paying a bill, saying no to a purchase, saving a little, giving.)

_____

_____

One Small Step I Will Take Next Week Is...

(Space for a simple action—track daily, adjust a category, make a payment, set up auto-transfer.)

_____

_____

My Prayer for My Finances This Week...

(Space to write a short prayer.)

_____

_____

You are not defined by your financial past.
With God, you are becoming a wise, faithful steward—
one honest look, one small decision, one obedient step at a time.

SECTION E:
The Pouring-From-Empty Giver – Relationships

This section is for you if your assessment highlighted relationships as a primary pain point —or if you know:

"I'm always there for everyone else, but I feel drained, unseen, or resentful. My relationships don't feel as healthy or mutual as I long for them to be."

This guide will help you invite God into your relationships, practice healthier boundaries, and move from pouring from empty to loving from a place of strength and wisdom.

Encouragement for the Pouring-From-Empty Giver

You care deeply about people.

You may be the one who:
- Shows up when others are in crisis
- Carries the emotional weight of the home, family, or friendships
- Says "yes" even when you're exhausted
- Keeps the peace, even when it costs you internally

But over time, that can leave you feeling:
- Drained and resentful
- Unseen or taken for granted
- Unsure how to say "no" without guilt
- Disconnected from your own needs and desires

If that's you, hear this:
Your compassion is a gift from God.
But He never asked you to be everyone's Savior.

MATTHEW 11:28–30
"Come to me, all you who are weary and burdened, and I will give you rest... For my yoke is easy and my burden is light."

GALATIANS 6:2, 5
"Carry each other's burdens... for each one should carry their own load."

PROVERBS 4:23
"Above all else, guard your heart, for everything you do flows from it."

You are called to love others—but you are also called to guard your heart, honor your limits, and let God be God.

- *In your closest relationships (family, friends, church, work), where do you feel most drained? Where do you feel most supported?*

_____

_____

_____

_____

- *If you're honest, what do you wish could change in your relationships right now?*

_____

_____

_____

_____

HONEST CHECK-IN:
Your Relationships Today

This is your space to tell the truth about how your relationships feel—without blaming or shaming yourself.

RATE EACH FROM 1-10 (1 = VERY POOR, 10 = EXCELLENT):

*Sense of being emotionally supported:*_____

Ability to say "no" without guilt: _____

Balance between giving and receiving in your relationships: _____

Health of communication (honesty, respect, listening): _____

Alignment between your relationships and your values/faith: _____

- *Where do you feel like you're "pouring from empty" the most? (Home, work, church, extended family, friendships?)*

  _____

  _____

  _____

- *What patterns do you notice in yourself—people-pleasing, avoiding conflict, over-functioning, withdrawing, etc.?*

  _____

  _____

  _____

- *Where do you already see signs of healthy, life-giving connection?*

  _____

  _____

  _____

Journaling Prompt

- *If your heart could speak about your relationships right now, what would it say?*

_____

_____

_____

_____

_____

_____

_____

_____

_____

_____

_____

_____

_____

_____

_____

_____

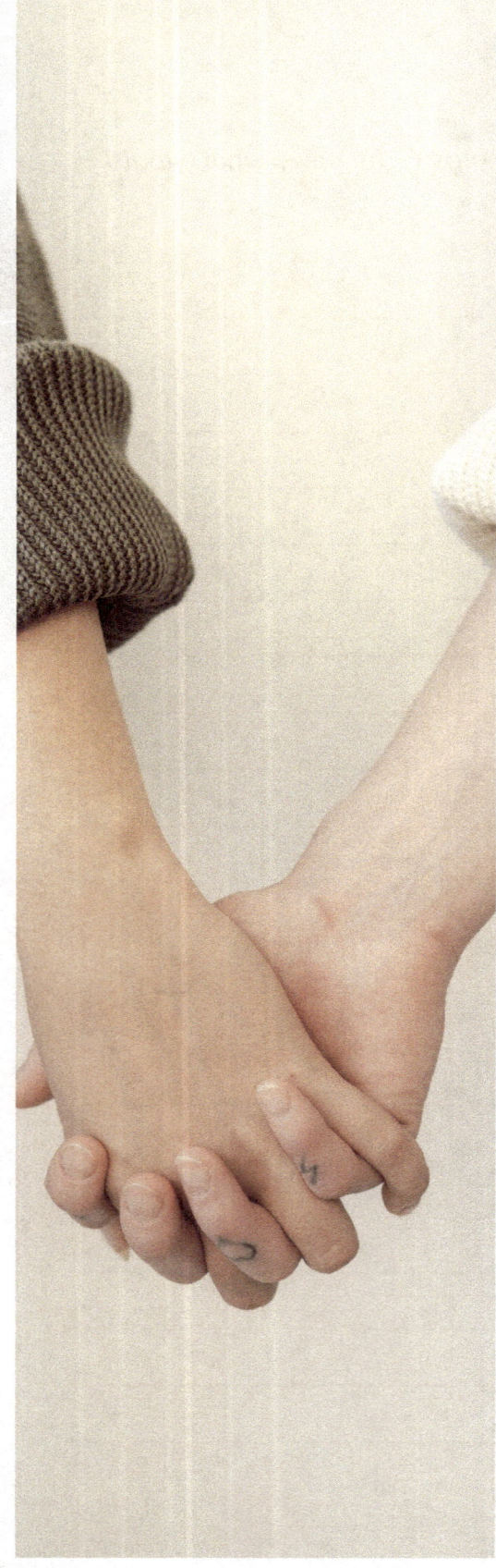

TINY SHIFTS, BIG IMPACT:
Relationship Habit

You don't need to fix every relationship overnight.

You need a few **tiny, intentional shifts** in how you show up, communicate, and care for yourself and others.

Use this as a **menu**. Circle or highlight what fits your season.

CONNECTION & PRESENCE
- Put your phone away for 15-20 minutes during a key daily moment (dinner, bedtime, car ride).
- Ask one meaningful question a day: "How are you really?"
- Schedule one intentional connection each week (coffee, walk, call, date night, game night).

BOUNDARIES & SAYING NO
- Practice one simple boundary sentence: "I'd love to help, but I can't do that right now."
- Before saying "yes," pause and ask: "Do I actually have the time/energy for this?"
- Choose one area where you will stop over-explaining your "no."

HONEST COMMUNICATION
- Pray before a hard conversation: "Lord, give me grace and truth."
- Use "I feel..." statements instead of blame (e.g., "I feel overwhelmed when...").
- After conflict, reflect: "What did I learn about myself? What could I try differently next time?"

SELF-CARE IN RELATIONSHIPS
- Take a 10-15 minute "reset" alone when you feel emotionally flooded.
- Do one thing each week that fills your cup (walk, hobby, reading, quiet time) without apologizing for it.
- Ask for help once a week, even in a small way.

PRAYER & RELEASE
- Regularly pray: "Lord, show me what's mine to carry and what's Yours."
- Release specific people into God's hands instead of trying to fix them.
- Pray blessing over someone who frustrates you (even if your feelings haven't caught up yet).

Which 2–4 tiny relationship habits from this list feel most realistic and needed for you right now?

_____

_____

_____

_____

_____

_____

_____

_____

Choose Your Relationship Focus

Now we'll bring Part Three's framework into your Pouring-From-Empty Giver focus.

*Based on my honest check-in and my 90-day vision, my **one main 90-day relationship goal** is...*

_____

_____

_____

_____

_____

❖

Examples:
"Have one intentional, distraction-free connection each week with my spouse/child/friend for the next 90 days."
"Practice saying 'no' at least once a week when something is beyond my capacity."
"Initiate one honest, grace-filled conversation about a recurring issue in a key relationship in the next 90 days."
"Build one new life-giving friendship or re-engage with a healthy relationship over the next 90 days."

MONTHLY MILESTONES
My 90-Day Goal & Monthly Milestones

MONTH 1
By the end of Month 1, I will...
(Example: identify key relationships to focus on, practice one new boundary or connection habit.)

_____

_____

_____

_____

MONTH 2
By the end of Month 2, I will...
(Example: have had several intentional connections or one important conversation.)

_____

_____

_____

_____

MONTH 3
By the end of Month 3, I will...
(Example: notice a shift in how I feel—less resentful, more honest, more connected.)

_____

_____

_____

_____

1-3 HEALTH REALTIONSHIP STACKS

Use the formula below to write 4 habit Stacks:

HABIT 1:

After I _____ ,

I will _____ .

HABIT 2:

After I _____ ,

I will _____ .

HABIT 3:

After I _____ ,

I will _____ .

Examples (she can copy or adapt):

After we sit down for dinner, I will put my phone away for the first 20 minutes.
After I feel that first wave of overwhelm, I will take 3 deep breaths and ask, "Lord, what's mine to carry here?"
After church on Sunday, I will send one encouraging text to a friend or family member.
After I put the kids to bed, I will spend 10 minutes connecting with my spouse or a close friend (talk, text, or call).

Journaling Prompt

- *How do these small habits move you from "pouring from empty" toward loving others from a place of fullness, honesty, and partnership with God?*

_____

_____

_____

_____

_____

_____

_____

_____

_____

_____

_____

_____

_____

_____

_____

_____

_____

_____

_____

_____

Stretched Steward Weekly Check-In

Sections:

This Week, I Nurtured My Relationships By...

(Space to list 3–5 ways she showed up with presence, honesty, or boundaries.)

_____

_____

This Week Was Hard Relationally Because...

(Space to be honest about conflict, disappointment, loneliness, or overload.)

_____

_____

I Felt Most Connected or Seen When...

(Space to reflect on moments of genuine connection.)

_____

_____

One Small Step I Will Take Next Week Is...

(Space for a simple action—plan a connection, set a boundary, ask for help, have a conversation.)

_____

_____

My Prayer for My Relationships This Week...

(Space to write a short prayer.)

_____

_____

You are not called to disappear in your relationships.
You are called to love others as you love yourself—
with truth, grace, and healthy limits, as you walk with God one small step at a time.

PART FIVE:
The Overloaded Overcomer Path

This part is for the woman who reads through this workbook and thinks:

"It's not just one area. It's all of them."

If your assessment pointed to the **Overloaded Overcomer**, or if your heart just knows that label fits, this section is for you.

You are not weak. You are not a failure. You are a strong, resilient woman who has been in survival mode for a long time. This path is here to help you move from **overloaded** to **ordered**, one gentle step at a time.

A Letter to the Overloaded Overcomer

Dear Overloaded Overcomer,

You are the woman who keeps going.

You show up when you're exhausted.
You hold things together when you feel like you're falling apart.
You carry responsibilities, emotions, and burdens that most people never see.

You are the one who:
- Figures it out when there's no clear answer
- Steps in when someone else drops the ball
- Holds space for other people's pain, even when your own heart is aching
- Keeps the house, the job, the kids, the ministry, the friendships, the appointments, the bills—moving

You have survived things that would have taken someone else out.
But somewhere along the way, "overcomer" turned into "overloaded."

You may feel:
- Like your mind never stops spinning
- Like your body is tired all the time
- Like your faith is hanging on by a thread
- Like your relationships are strained or shallow
- Like your finances are a constant background stress
- Like you don't even know where to begin, because everything feels urgent

If that's you, I want you to hear this:
God is not standing over you with a clipboard, asking why you haven't "fixed" your life yet.

He is sitting beside you, with compassion in His eyes, saying:
"Daughter, I see how much you've been carrying.
You don't have to hold it all by yourself anymore.
Let's lay some things down. Let's choose where to start—together."

You are not behind.
You are not too much.
You are not too far gone.
You are loved, seen, and held—even here, in the middle of the mess.

This path is not about becoming superhuman. It's about learning how to:
- Put down what was never yours to carry
- Let God reorder what's on your plate
- Focus on one area at a time, with grace
- Build a life that is sustainable, not just survivable

You don't have to do this alone.
You don't have to do this perfectly.
You just have to be willing to start.

With you,

Candice and Liz

Journaling Prompt

- *As you read this letter, what words or phrases hit you the hardest? Why?*

_____

_____

_____

_____

_____

- *Where do you most feel the "overloaded" part of you right now—in your body, your thoughts, your emotions, your relationships, your schedule?*

_____

_____

_____

_____

_____

- *If Jesus could sit with you on your couch today, what do you wish He would say or do for you?*

_____

_____

_____

_____

_____

PRIORITIZING WHEN EVERYTHING *Feels Urgent*

When everything feels urgent, your nervous system goes into survival mode. You're not "crazy" or "dramatic"—you're overloaded.

That overload often shows up in patterns like:

- **Freeze**
  - "It's all too much. I can't deal with any of it."
  - (You shut down, numb out, or avoid decisions.)

- **Flight**
  - "If I stay busy enough or distracted enough, maybe I won't have to feel this."
  - (You overwork, over-scroll, over-schedule, or constantly escape into activity.)

- **Fight**
  - "I have to push harder and control everything."
  - (You get tense, irritable, controlling, or harsh with yourself and others.)

- **Fawn**
  - "I'll just keep taking care of everyone else and ignore my own needs."
  - (You people-please, say yes when you mean no, and disappear inside others' expectations.)

- **Flail**
  - "I'll try to fix everything at once for three days, then crash."
  - (You launch into an intense overhaul, then burn out and feel like a failure.)

None of these responses mean you're broken. They mean you've been trying to survive. This section is about gently shifting from **reaction** to **prayerful priority**.

STEP 1:

Name Your Life Areas Honestly

First, let's get everything out of your head and onto paper.

Write each area, then rank them from 1–5 based on how painful or unsustainable they feel right now.

1 = MOST URGENT / MOST PAINFUL, 5 = LEAST URGENT RIGHT NOW:

- *Faith (my walk with God):* ___
- *Health (body, energy, rest, emotions):* ___
- *Finances (money, debt, bills, income):* ___
- *Relationships (home, work, church, friendships):* ___
- *Personal Development & Purpose (growth, calling, direction):* ___

As you look at your rankings, what stands out to you?

_____

_____

_____

_____

Is there an area that feels like it's "screaming the loudest"?

_____

_____

_____

_____

Is there an area that's been easy to ignore but is quietly hurting you?

_____

_____

_____

_____

If you had to describe your life in one sentence right now, what would it be?

_____

_____

_____

_____

STEP 2:

"If God Said Start Here..." Exercise

This is where we move from **pressure to prayerful priority**.

Take a deep breath. Imagine Jesus sitting across from you, looking at your life with love and clarity.

Close your eyes for a moment and picture Jesus looking at your life—your calendar, your body, your bank account, your relationships, your thoughts.

- If He gently put His hand on **one** area of your life and said,

- "Daughter, let's start here,"

- which area do you sense He would choose?

Write it down:

- *"I sense God inviting me to start with: _____."*

Why do you think He might be highlighting this area first?

_____

_____

_____

_____

If this area began to heal or strengthen, how might it create a ripple effect in the rest of your life?

_____

_____

_____

_____

Prayer

*"Lord, I don't know where to start.
Show me where You want to begin.
I trust Your order more than my overwhelm."*

YOU ARE NOT FAILING BY NOT FIXING EVERYTHING.

YOU ARE BEING WISE BY LETTING GOD SET THE ORDER OF YOUR HEALING.

STEP 3:

Triage Questions for Overloaded Seasons

If you're still unsure where to start, use these triage questions:

Where am I in the most immediate danger of burning out or breaking down?
(This often points to Health or Relationships.)

_____

_____

_____

_____

Where am I feeling the loudest, constant stress or fear?
(This often points to Finances, Health, or Relationships.)

_____

_____

_____

_____

Where do I feel the most spiritually numb or disconnected?
(This often points to Faith.)

_____

_____

_____

_____

Where do I feel like I've completely lost myself?
(This often points to Personal Development & Purpose.)

_____

_____

_____

_____

Which area, if it improved even a little, would make everything else feel more manageable?

Write your answer:

- "If this area improved even a little, it would make the biggest difference:

  _____

  _____

  _____."

Your One-Area-At-a-Time Plan

This is your permission slip and your plan:

You will focus on **one primary area at a time**—not because the others don't matter, but because you matter, and you are not a machine.

Choosing Your First Focus

Using your rankings, triage answers, and the "If God Said Start Here…" exercise, choose your first focus area for the next 90 days.

For the next 90 days, my primary focus area will be: _____

because: _____

THEN:

- **Turn to the corresponding Focus Area Guide:**
  - Weary Warrior → Health & Wellness
  - Hidden Heroine → Personal Development & Purpose
  - Hungry Heart → Faith Life
  - Stretched Steward → Finances
  - Pouring-From-Empty Giver → Relationships

- **Use that guide to:**
  - Set your 90-day goal
  - Choose 1–3 tiny habits
  - Use the weekly check-in pages

> YOU CAN JOT DOWN IDEAS FOR THE OTHER AREAS, BUT YOU ARE ONLY ACTIVELY WORKING ON ONE IN THIS SEASON. THAT'S NOT NEGLECT—THAT'S WISDOM.

Guardrails for Overloaded Seasons

Because you're used to doing too much, you'll need some **guardrails** to protect yourself from slipping back into overload.

Think of these as agreements between you and God for this season.

GUARDRAIL #1: ONE MAIN FOCUS

Statement:

"For this 90-day season, I will only have one primary growth focus. I may notice other areas, but I will not try to overhaul them all at once."

Space to initial or sign:

_____

_____

What fears come up when you think about focusing on just one area?

_____

_____

_____

What might God be inviting you to trust about His timing and care for the other areas?

_____

_____

_____

GUARDRAIL #2: TINY STEPS, NOT HUGE LEAPS

Statement:

"When I feel the urge to do something extreme (all-or-nothing plans, huge overhauls), I will pause and choose a smaller, sustainable step instead."

What is one "extreme" pattern you tend to default to when you're overwhelmed? (Example: starting a strict diet, planning a massive declutter, making big promises you can't keep.)

_____

_____

_____

What is a gentler, smaller alternative you can choose instead?

_____

_____

_____

EXAMPLE:
Extreme: "I'm going to wake up at 4 a.m. every day and work out for an hour."
Gentle: "I will walk for 10-15 minutes 3 days a week."

GUARDRAIL #3: BUILT-IN REST

Statement:

"I will build in at least one small pocket of rest each week (even 30–60 minutes) where I am not fixing, planning, or producing."

What could your weekly rest pocket look like in this season?

(*Time, place, activity—e.g., a walk, a bath, reading, quiet with God, sitting outside.*)

_____

_____

_____

When will it happen? (Day/time): _____

REST IS NOT A REWARD FOR FINISHING EVERYTHING.
IT IS PART OF HOW GOD HEALS, RESTORES, AND
STRENGTHENS YOU.

GUARDRAIL #4: ASK FOR HELP

Statement:

"I will not try to carry everything alone.

I will ask for help—from God and from at least one trusted person."

Who is one person you can invite into this journey (friend, spouse, mentor, coach, group)?

_____

_____

_____

What is one specific way you can ask for help this month?

(Example: "Can we check in once a week?" "Can you help with the kids one afternoon?"

"Can you pray with me about my finances?")

_____

_____

_____

Overloaded → Ordered Roadmap (90-Day Cycle):

PAUSE & TELL THE TRUTH
Use the Overloaded Overcomer section to name where you are.

PRAY & PRIORITIZE
Rank your life areas.
Ask, "If God said start here, where would it be?"

CHOOSE ONE FOCUS AREA
Pick Faith, Health, Finances, Relationships, or Purpose.
Turn to that Focus Area Guide.

SET ONE 90-DAY GOAL + 1-3 TINY HABITS
Use Part Three + your Focus Area Guide.

WALK IT OUT WITH GUARDRAILS
One main focus.
Tiny steps, not huge leaps.
Weekly rest.
Ask for help.

REVIEW & REPEAT
At the end of 90 days, reflect.
Decide whether to stay with the same area or shift to another.

You are not meant to live in constant crisis mode.

With God, you can move from:
Overloaded → Ordered
Surviving → Stabilizing → Strengthening

Not in one weekend.
Not in one sprint.
But one area, one decision, one small, faithful step at a time.

You are an overcomer.
Now, by God's grace, you're learning how not to be overloaded.

This is your new way forward.

PART SIX
The Overloaded Overcomer Path

This part is where you pause, look back, and notice:

- What has actually changed
- How God has met you in this process
- How your focus area has affected the rest of your life
- Where He might be leading you next

Use these pages at the end of each month and again at the end of your 90-day journey.

MONTH 1 REFLECTION

What Changed This Month?
In my focus area, what changed this month—big or small?
(Think: thoughts, habits, emotions, circumstances.)

_____

_____

_____

_____

What new habits did I actually practice? Which ones felt most natural? Which ones were hardest?

_____

_____

_____

_____

Did anything shift in my energy, mood, schedule, or relationships because of these changes?

_____

_____

_____

_____

WHERE DID I SEE GOD AT WORK?

Where did I sense God's presence, guidance, or comfort this month?

_____

_____

_____

_____

Did any Scriptures, sermons, conversations, or "coincidences" stand out as God speaking to me?

_____

_____

_____

_____

Where did I experience unexpected grace, provision, or breakthrough?

_____

_____

_____

_____

PROGRESS, NOT PERFECTION

Where did I struggle, fall off, or feel stuck this month?

_____

_____

_____

_____

What did those moments reveal about what I need (rest, support, structure, healing, boundaries)?

_____

_____

_____

_____

If I look at this month through the lens of grace, what am I proud of?

_____

_____

_____

_____

ONE ADJUSTMENT FOR NEXT MONTH

- One small adjustment I will make next month is...

_____

_____

_____."

MONTH 2 REFLECTION

What Changed This Month?
In my focus area, what changed this month—big or small?
(Think: thoughts, habits, emotions, circumstances.)

_____

_____

_____

_____

What new habits did I actually practice? Which ones felt most natural? Which ones were hardest?

_____

_____

_____

_____

Did anything shift in my energy, mood, schedule, or relationships because of these changes?

_____

_____

_____

_____

WHERE DID I SEE GOD AT WORK?

Where did I sense God's presence, guidance, or comfort this month?

_____

_____

_____

_____

Did any Scriptures, sermons, conversations, or "coincidences" stand out as God speaking to me?

_____

_____

_____

_____

Where did I experience unexpected grace, provision, or breakthrough?

_____

_____

_____

_____

PROGRESS, NOT PERFECTION

Where did I struggle, fall off, or feel stuck this month?

_____

_____

_____

_____

What did those moments reveal about what I need (rest, support, structure, healing, boundaries)?

_____

_____

_____

_____

If I look at this month through the lens of grace, what am I proud of?

_____

_____

_____

_____

ONE ADJUSTMENT FOR NEXT MONTH

- One small adjustment I will make next month is...

_____

_____

_____."

MONTH 3 REFLECTION

What Changed This Month?
In my focus area, what changed this month—big or small?
(Think: thoughts, habits, emotions, circumstances.)

_____

_____

_____

_____

What new habits did I actually practice? Which ones felt most natural? Which ones were hardest?

_____

_____

_____

_____

Did anything shift in my energy, mood, schedule, or relationships because of these changes?

_____

_____

_____

_____

WHERE DID I SEE GOD AT WORK?

Where did I sense God's presence, guidance, or comfort this month?

_____
_____
_____
_____

Did any Scriptures, sermons, conversations, or "coincidences" stand out as God speaking to me?

_____
_____
_____
_____

Where did I experience unexpected grace, provision, or breakthrough?

_____
_____
_____
_____

PROGRESS, NOT PERFECTION

Where did I struggle, fall off, or feel stuck this month?

_____
_____
_____
_____

What did those moments reveal about what I need (rest, support, structure, healing, boundaries)?

_____

_____

_____

_____

If I look at this month through the lens of grace, what am I proud of?

_____

_____

_____

_____

ONE ADJUSTMENT FOR NEXT MONTH

- One small adjustment I will make next month is...

_____

_____

_____."

Whole-Life Reflection

Use this section at the end of your 90-day cycle to see the bigger picture.

HOW THIS FOCUS AREA AFFECTED THE REST OF MY LIFE

My primary focus area this season was: _____

Then reflect on each area (with space under each):

- *Faith – What shifted in my relationship with God because of this focus?*
- *Health – Did anything change in my body, energy, or emotional capacity?*
- *Finances – Did my money stress, awareness, or stewardship shift at all?*
- *Relationships – Did this focus affect how I show up with others?*
- *Personal Development & Purpose – Did I gain any clarity, confidence, or direction?*

What surprised you most about how working on one area affected the others?

_____

_____

_____

WHAT GOD HAS DONE IN THIS SEASON

If you had to name 3–5 ways God has worked in you this season, what would they be?

(Think: healing, perspective, courage, peace, new habits, restored hope, conviction.)

_____

_____

_____

What prayers did He answer—clearly or quietly?

_____

_____

_____

What prayers are still in process?

_____

_____

_____

Testimony Snapshot

Imagine you're sharing a short testimony with a friend about these last 90 days. How would you finish this sentence?

"Over the last few months, God has...

_____

_____

_____

_____

_____

_____

_____

_____

_____

_____."

Looking Ahead

This section helps you decide what's next and commit to a simple plan.

CHOOSING YOUR NEXT FOCUS AREA

- ***As you look ahead to the next 90 days, what do you sense God highlighting as your next focus?***
  - *Stay with the same area and go deeper?*
  - *Shift to a new area (another profile)?*
  - *Maintain a few habits here while gently adding one new area?*

_____

_____

_____

Which area feels most important for your next season, and why?

_____

_____

_____

"For my next 90 days, my primary focus will be _____

because _____"

YOU CAN REVISIT:

- Your original assessment
- Your Overloaded Overcomer section (if that's you)
- Any areas that still feel especially painful, neglected, or ready for growth

CHOOSING YOUR NEXT FOCUS AREA

One habit I will continue from this last season is...

_____

_____

_____

One new step I will add in the next season is...

_____

_____

_____

One expectation, pressure, or pattern I will intentionally release is...

_____

_____

_____

One way I will invite support (friend, group, coach, church, mentor) is...

_____

_____

_____

NEXT 90 DAYS SNAPSHOT

- Focus Area: _____

- Main 90-Day Goal: _____

- Top 3 Habits I'm Committing To:
    - a.
    - b.
    - c.

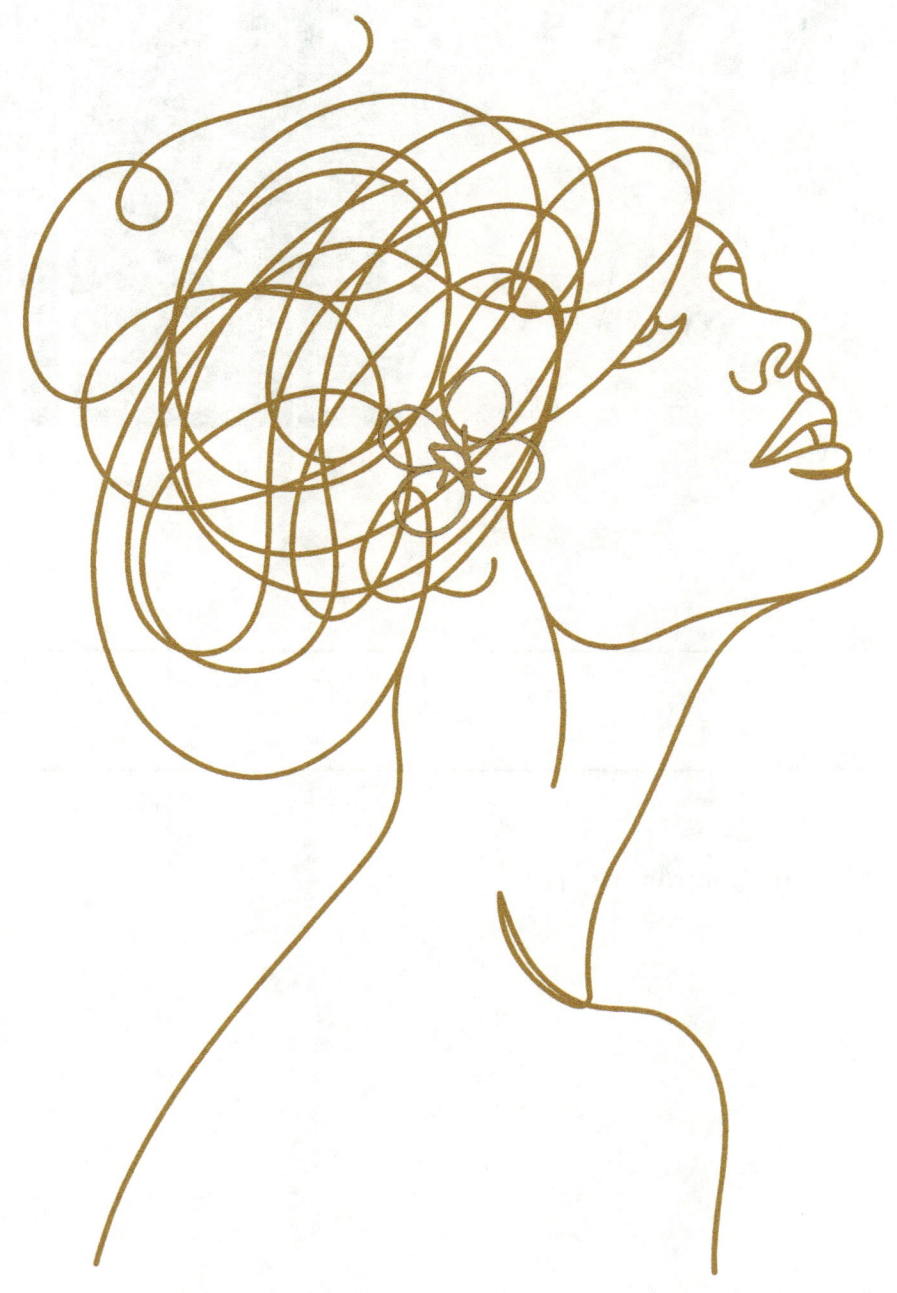

PART SEVEN
Support & Community

You were never meant to walk out a whole-life makeover alone.

This part is here to remind you that:
- You don't have to carry everything by yourself
- You grow faster and steadier with support
- There are women and coaches ready to walk alongside you

You Don't Have to Do This Alone

THE POWER OF COMMUNITY & ACCOUNTABILITY

Change is personal, but it's not meant to be isolated.

When you invite safe people into your journey, you gain:
- **Encouragement** – Someone to remind you who you are when you forget
- **Perspective** – Another set of eyes to help you see what you can't see yet
- **Accountability** – Gentle check-ins that keep you moving when you'd normally quit
- **Prayer Covering** – Sisters who stand in the gap when you're tired or discouraged

Journaling Prompt

- *Who are 1-3 people in your life who feel safe, wise, or encouraging?*

_____

_____

_____

_____

_____

- *How could you invite them into your journey—prayer, check-ins, honest conversations, practical help?*

_____

_____

_____

_____

_____

- *What kind of support do you most need in this season—emotional, spiritual, practical, or all of the above?*

_____

_____

_____

_____

_____

How to Go Deeper

You've done beautiful work in these pages. If you sense God inviting you to go deeper, you don't have to figure it out on your own.

JOINING THE AURORA NETWORK COMMUNITY

Aurora Network exists to support women just like you—women who love Jesus, know they were made for more, and are ready to grow with support.

Inside the Aurora Network community, you'll find:
Christ-centered teaching and encouragement
A network of female Christian life coaches and mentors
Spaces to process your journey with other women who "get it"
Opportunities to go deeper in your faith, health, finances, relationships, and purpose

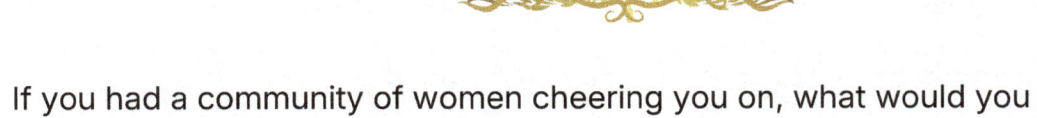

If you had a community of women cheering you on, what would you hope that space would give you?

_____

_____

_____

BOOKING A COACHING SESSION

Sometimes the most loving thing you can do for yourself is to sit down with someone who is trained to help you:
Untangle your thoughts
Clarify your next steps
Create a plan that fits your real life
Stay accountable with grace, not shame

A Christian life coach can help you:
Apply what you've started in this workbook to your unique season
Navigate complex situations (trauma, transitions, burnout, leadership, calling)
Build sustainable rhythms in your focus area (faith, health, finances, relationships, purpose)

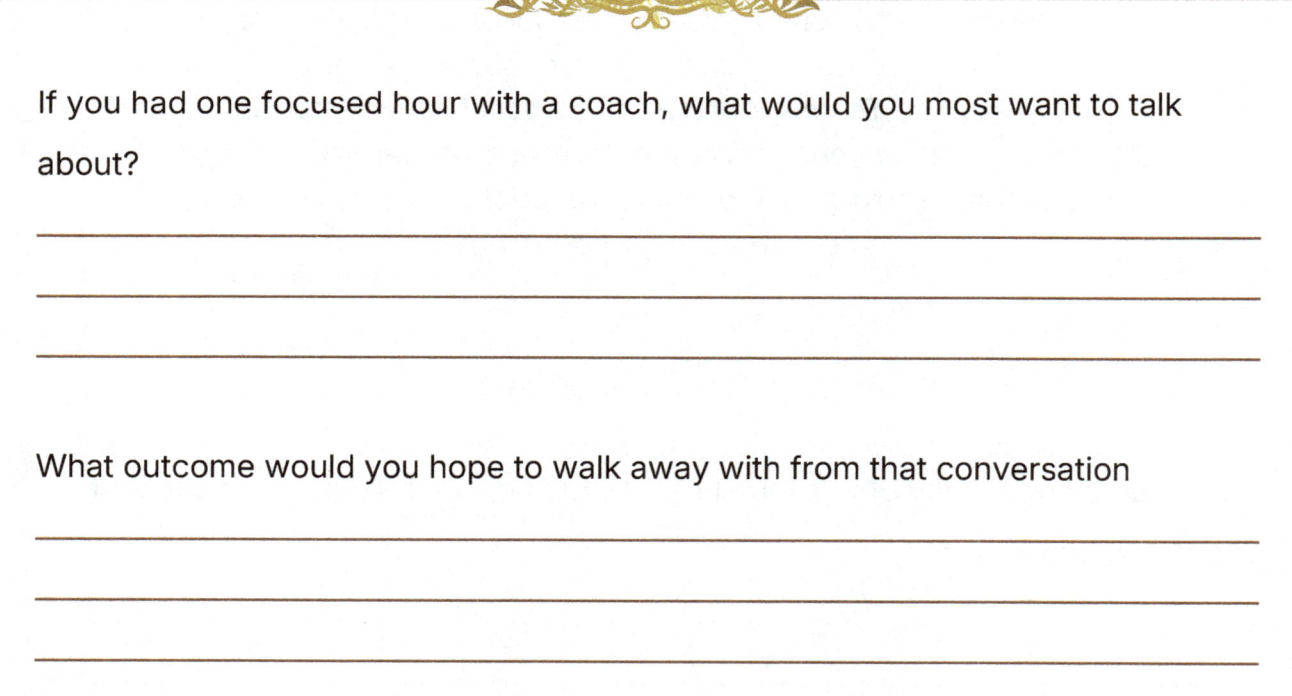

If you had one focused hour with a coach, what would you most want to talk about?

_____

_____

_____

What outcome would you hope to walk away with from that conversation

_____

_____

_____

What are you waiting for?

Book a clarity session
Join a group program or membership
Explore ongoing coaching in your focus area

[VISIT AURORA NETWORK.LIFE!]

Final Blessing

May you remember, in every season,
that you are not just a woman trying to get her life together—
you are a beloved daughter of the King.

May your heart stay soft to God's voice,
your steps be guided by His wisdom,
and your days be marked by grace, not pressure.

May you see His hand in your faith,
His strength in your body,
His provision in your finances,
His love in your relationships,
and His purpose in your work and calling.

When you feel behind,
may you hear Him whisper, "You're right on time with Me."
When you feel overwhelmed,
may you remember you can choose one small, faithful step.
When you feel alone,
may you sense His presence and remember you have sisters in this
journey.

Closing Prayer

Jesus, thank You for every woman who has walked through these pages.
You know her story, her scars, her strengths, and her secret hopes.

I ask that You would seal the work You've begun in her—
the shifts in her thinking,
the new habits,
the healing in her heart,
the courage to face what once felt impossible.

Lead her into the next season with clarity and peace.
Surround her with the right people,
the right support,
and the right opportunities.

Remind her, again and again,
that she is not behind,
not too much,
and not alone.

May her life become a living testimony
of Your grace, Your power, and Your faithfulness.

In Your name, Jesus, we pray.
Amen.

"DO NOT CONFORM TO THE PATTERN OF THIS WORLD, BUT BE TRANSFORMED BY THE RENEWING OF YOUR MIND. THEN YOU WILL BE ABLE TO TEST AND APPROVE WHAT GOD'S WILL IS—HIS GOOD, PLEASING AND PERFECT WILL."
– ROMANS 12:2 (NIV)